T0196411

TRAVELS WITH AN ARTIST

HELEN ANN LICHT

authorHOUSE®

AuthorHouse™
1663 Liberty Drive
Bloomington, IN 47403
www.authorhouse.com
Phone: 833-262-8899

Published by AuthorHouse 04/12/2021

ISBN: 978-1-6655-1669-3 (sc)
ISBN: 978-1-6655-1670-9 (e)

Introduction

The history I have written about has passed. I would hope the prejudices expressed are gone. I want to thank my family for everything they have done for me. Without their guidance, I would not be the person I am today. The book is also about my values.

I want to thank my husband, Norman, for his love, constant calmness, stability, and encouragement, allowing me to be who I am. I've had a wonderful life. This is a hard time, during the coronavirus pandemic, but it has enabled me to write this book.

Contents

The Goldsteins of Alaska

TWO CENTS PER ACRE FOR all of Alaska included mountains, glaciers, water, and trees. It was unexplored Russian territory when United States Secretary of State William H. Seward arranged for the $7,200,000 purchase in 1867.

Reuben Goldstein started a trading post in an Indian village named after the Tlingit Chief, Kowee Juneau, in 1882. Gold was discovered off Gastineau Channel in Gold Creek. A few prospectors set up a gold camp there in 1892. That gold rush brought many prospectors anxious to make their fortunes.

My great-grandfather, Reuben, was born in Kiev, Russia. The army conscription law in Russia said that if you were caught you had to serve in the army for the rest of your life. Reuben ran away as a youngster to find work in the fur markets of London There were rumors of a first wife along the way. He married Anna in London in the 1860s. She was from Gorodek, in the Ukraine, near Chernobyl, born of a mother from Spain..Rueben and Anna had eight children, three boys and five girls. The oldest, Charlie, was born in London. Next came Will and Isadore. The girls were Esther, Minnie, Flora, Mollie, and Belle. The family came via London to Winnipeg in 1877. Five of their children were born in Canada. Mollie, my grandmother, was at one time listed in the state records as the oldest living Jewish woman born in Winnipeg, Manitoba. Reuben's brother, Moses, was also in Canada, but there is little mention of him.

Reuben supported himself as a peddler (a common trade for Jewish immigrants of the day). In 1877, he was the first Jewish peddler to settle permanently in Manitoba. The

Manitoba Press reported his frequent departure by horse-drawn stagecoach on peddling jaunts in 1878. There was a Goldstein family listed among the founding members of the Rosh Pina Synagogue in Winnipeg.

As a young man, he sold some jewelry to workers laying the tracks along the Canadian railway line. He brought charges in the Winnipeg police court on March 6, 1879, against a railroader who assaulted him at Brouse's Hotel. Apparently, there were instances when ruffians made sport of his Jewish origin. In this case, it was a dispute about watches. The railroader accused him of having something to do with the crucifixion of Christ. Goldstein retorted sharply, and the railroader punched him in the head. The railroader was apparently remorseful and offered to compensate Reuben five dollars for the damage done to him. Reuben persisted in pressing the charges. The magistrate dismissed the case and charged the costs to Goldstein.

There was also a problem over a watch that Goldstein sold on the first installment plan in Manitoba. A customer tried to return the watch but couldn't because Reuben was traveling so much. Reuben's solicitors threatened a writ to get the watch back. They finally got it back but could not collect any of the money he was owed. A few other problems followed, according to the court records of the time. Reuben decided to leave peddling.

Next, he tried to establish himself as a hotelkeeper at St. Francois Xavier, Manitoba. He also dabbled in land speculation. He experimented with farming at Headingley, Manitoba, becoming the first Jewish farmer in the province. In 1885 the hotelkeeper-farmer-rancher became restless again. Still having the pioneer spirit, he emigrated to the United States.

In California he went into a salmon saltery business on the Sacramento River. The business failed, and he was broke again. There were stories of wonderful furs in Alaska, so Reuben and his oldest son, Charlie, who was just sixteen years old, set out.

The first Goldstein business in Alaska was on the banks of the Gastineau Channel, overlooking Juneau Bay. South Franklin Street in Juneau is there today. The store was built of logs, and the family lived upstairs. Since the Goldsteins were a large family, they slept two children to a bed. They placed barrels under the roof to collect rainwater to use for everything but cooking and drinking. The drinking water came from a nearby freshwater stream. One winter a snowstorm barred them from their home for an entire month.

"Outhouses, called bathhouses, were commonplace," according to my great-aunt Belle. "They had a bathhouse on the back porch." Aunt Belle remembered "bear hides for carpets on the dining room floor and glossy sea-otter pelts draped from hooks along the walls."

The indigenous people came with their canoes stacked high with goods to barter with the Goldsteins. In addition to furs, there was also the possibility of family prospecting. With the discovery of gold in the Klondike, the Goldstein family business grew from fur trading into a large mercantile business supplying the prospectors, the tourists, and the locals. Anna seemed to be the person running the store. Often Reuben and his sons went by dog caravan and sleds into the interior of Alaska to trade for more furs.

I have heard Mollie, my grandmother, tell stories of the storms in Juneau. The Goldstein warehouse was on stilts (piers) in the bay. It was entered by a bridge over the water. Every morning Reuben got up early to see if the warehouse was still there or hit by icebergs and floating away down Gastineau Channel. That really happened to them—Mollie remembered watching the wooden warehouse slip off its piers and float away. I never heard how or whether it was rescued.

Native people included the Tlingit and the Haidas. Mollie used to tell me stories of the Chilkat people who came from Taku, near the glacier, in long canoes. The indigenous people did not speak English, but they knew how to trade. My great uncles learned to count and communicate with them in their language, Tlingit (Klingit). They would trade in the Goldstein store along with the prospectors. Merchandise included imported Hudson Bay blankets and leaf tobacco for rolling. Indian curios were sold on the side of the store facing the bay. Aunt Belle told me of a wizened, blanket-covered native with twenty-dollar gold pieces in his wrinkled mouth who spit them out on the counter in payment for his goods.

Juneau could only be reached by boat, because high mountains and glaciers surrounded it. The one boat each month that rounded the Gastineau Channel would blow a loud whistle, even during the middle of the night. Upon hearing the whistle, everybody would run to the banks. The Indian people would run down the dirt or wooden streets yelling in Tlingit, "The steamer is coming. The steamer is coming," a continuous chant at the top of their voices. They would run to the slanted dirt banks at the shore of the channel and place their wares on top of boxes or on the ground to wait for the early prospectors and tourists to disembark and buy their moccasins, blankets, ivory, and decorative beadwork. When the boat was not in the harbor, they could be seen sitting on the wooden streets and in their homes making their moccasins, sewing beaded items, and sculpting ivory whale's teeth and bones.

Image: Charles (b. 18 or 19 Aug 1868) not in picture. Standing: Minnie (b. 24 Mar 1875), Flora (1873), and Esther (1871), Reuben (b. 22 Feb 1833), and Anna Ephraims Goldstein (b. 18 Aug 1847) holding Molly (b. 22 Feb 1880), Will (1877), and Isadore (b. 1 Feb 1883). Belle (b. 27 Mar 1885 or 1886 in Seattle, not born in this picture) California 1884

Later these same indigenous people sold their wares to my Aunt Belle Simpson when she started her own curio store, the Nugget Shop. They would barter white or beige fur-topped leather moccasins sewn with colored beads, woven grass baskets, carved walrus tusks, bearskin rugs, pipes, and handmade jewelry. Some of the handwork was the same as that sold in the general store by Reuben and Anna.

The family retained most of its Jewish customs. Frozen kosher meat was sent to Juneau by boat from the one kosher butcher in Seattle. Because of the cold climate there was natural refrigeration. The trading post was closed on every Jewish holiday. Sometimes the holidays were celebrated by the family in Seattle at the first orthodox shul, Biker Cholom. Reuben died in Juneau in 1900 and was buried in the orthodox cemetery in Seattle. He left a wife and eight children.

Charlie (Rueben's oldest child)

My great-uncle, Charlie, became a successful fur trader and merchant. At one time he had a fur farm and raised animals in cages. Once the animals caught a disease, and all of them died. He was a thirty-third degree Mason, quite an honor in his time. He founded the Goldstein Improvement Company for his many business ventures. He

Charlie Goldstein 1930

had a large retail shop in his building, which later included the Baranof Hotel, where he lived.

Uncle Charlie went fur hunting by dogsled. As soon as small propeller-driven planes were invented, hunting and flying became his way of life. In the winter he would fly into the interior of Alaska; the ski planes landed in the snow. Charlie's brother, Will, was killed in a hunting accident, shot by his own gun as he attempted to climb over the stump of a tree.

Charlie married Laura Goldberg of San Francisco. They had three children, Marie, Marion (Mickey), and Alvin. Mickey was killed in a small-plane crash in Alaska in 1933, five days before I was born. My mother was not informed about the death of her favorite uncle until my birth was over. Marie graduated from the University of California. She married John Dolginer, a fur merchant and lived a long life in Beverly Hills. They had two children, daughter Joan and son Charles, and six grandchildren. Joan was a geriatric social worker married to

Mel Adler. They have five children: Susan, Greg, Judith, and Karen. Charles is a lawyer. He has two children, Samantha and Amy. Together they maintain a summer home in Alaska.

Alvin and his wife, Camille Rosenberg, had one child, Aileen Ann. While a student at Stanford, she married a fellow student, Leonard Pockman. He became a professor of physics at San Francisco State University, and she became a social worker. They lived in a lovely home on Palm Drive in San Francisco. Leonard, along with his friends, refused to sign the loyalty oath imposed on academics by Senator Joe McCarthy in the 1950s and was dismissed from his position during the communist scare. Aileen Ann admitted to me before she died that she, too, was a member of the Communist Party. Uncle Charlie sent her to Stanford, but he left her only one dollar in his will. Leonard became very sick, and he and Aileen Ann lost their beautiful home. After lying on his back for years, Leonard died at a very young age. My Aunt Ruby and I visited Aileen Ann often in her tiny apartment in Palo Alto. I think Aunt Ruby even helped her financially. Aileen Ann was one of my most interesting relatives because of her educated, liberal, and critical views of our country. She had a sad life and became sick and unable to work. She had one son, Jack. Her gold Tlingit bracelet is in the Alaska Historical Museum in Juneau.

Isadore Goldstein Alaska 1919

Isadore

My great-uncle Isadore Goldstein was born in San Francisco on Minna Street behind the Palace Hotel in 1882, just before the family left for Alaska. Reuben, and later Isadore, got into the fish business. Eventually my Uncle Iz owned a fishing fleet and a fisherman's supply business on the main street in Juneau. Alaska's waters were full of fish. There were large coho salmon, halibut, and huge crabs, which were caught in giant steel-wired crab traps right off the shore. In 1910, while still a young man, Izzy left the business in his sister's hands for two years to become a miner when there was a gold strike in Iditerod, up the Yukon River. He didn't strike gold, but he opened a store there. Later he bought a mink ranch. He, too, put concrete over the grass. The animals all died from lack of roughage. He and his nephew, Mickey, discovered oil in the interior of Alaska, but they didn't have the money to develop it.

Uncle Izzy joined the army in World War 1. He served in Europe and returned in 1919. Iz was a bachelor until the age of forty-four. In 1926 he married twenty-year-old Carol Kahn of San Francisco after a three-day courtship in Alaska; Carol had come to Juneau on a trip with her close friend Marie Goldstein. Carol and Iz lived in a flat above the fishing and tackle store on Front Street, the wooden street that went by the store to the Indian village.

Uncle Iz served as mayor of Juneau for six terms. He also served two years on the city council. He was asked to run, he said, "because of the skullduggery in the government." He was a man of the people, unimpressed by titles and prestige. Under his popular leadership, concrete sidewalks were built as well as the first children's playground in Alaska, the Evergreen Bowl. He also helped obtain WPA funds to rebuild the docks.

In 1923, during the presidency of Warren G. Harding, Uncle Izzy's picture was taken with President Harding on the steps of the governor's mansion. That was the year of the first presidential trip to Alaska, just before Harding was killed at the Palace Hotel in San Francisco.

Uncle Iz and Aunt Carol were the last people to see Will Rogers and Wiley Post before their small airplane crashed in Point Barrows, Alaska. Aunt Carol told me Will's last words to her when he boarded the plane were, "You are going to need a can opener to open this thing up." There is a picture in the Will Rogers Museum in Colorado Springs, Colorado, of Uncle Iz handing the keys to the city of Juneau to Will on that fateful day.

Uncle Iz retired to San Francisco, where he lived with his wife and his son Robert. He died in 1959, far away from his beloved Juneau. Bob graduated from San Jose State. He married Helen, a nurse. He was in the insurance business as well as being a volunteer firefighter. They had one daughter. Bob died within the last five years.

Belle Simpson (The Belle of Alaska)

Seattle was where Anna went for her confinement for the birth of their youngest child, my great-aunt Belle. Nevertheless, Belle claimed she was the first Jewish child born in Alaska.

Hootchnoo and Hotcakes was the melodrama that was performed for tourists in Juneau for about twenty years. The main characters were Anna Goldstein, Reuben Goldstein, and baby Belle Goldstein. Belle was three years old when the natives captured her. The curly-haired child was in the back of their canoe behind some pelts as they disembarked. She called out, "Izzy, William, Charlie," and the brothers went out in a row boat. Charlie trained his rifle on the canoe and ordered it back to shore. This adventure was later memorialized for the visiting tourists.

Belle was at one time considered the most beautiful girl in Alaska. She met her husband, Robert Simpson, in Iditerod, where he had a jewelry and optometry store. Although he was not Jewish, Belle always maintained her Jewishness. She later donated the land for the temple, Congregation Sukkat Shalom, in Juneau and was present at the bar mitzvah of Alan Gross, the first bar mitzvah to be held in Juneau, in 1975. It was performed by Rabbi Morris Hershman, a visiting rabbi from California. My modern painting of Masada hangs there now.

The Nugget Shop was the largest Alaskan curio shop in Juneau. Robert Simpson had his optometry office there. In addition to curios and optometry, the Nugget Shop carried native jewelry. Belle is credited with the discovery and promotion of Sydney Laurence, the famous painter of colorful, realistic Alaskan landscapes and life. Some of Sydney Laurence's paintings hang in the Juneau Art Museum courtesy of Belle. I inherited three Sydney Laurence paintings from my family. Only my son Bruce and his wife were interested, so they took one, and I sold the other two.

I was in high school when I went to Juneau with my grandmother, Mollie, on the *Inland Passage* in 1949. I still remember Juneau when the boats came in at midnight. The entire town would open up under the leadership of Belle and serve the tourists as if it were the middle of the day. The summer I was in Alaska, I was allowed to work in the Nugget Shop. Authentic native crafts and art was sold there, including ivory, baleen baskets, woven blankets, masks, miniature totem poles, and fine jewelry. When Aunt Belle heard one of my customers was Mrs. Scranton of Scranton, Pennsylvania, she immediately relieved me of my duty and took over.

Whenever Governor Greuning entertained visiting navy officers in whites and uniforms from one of the military ships visiting Juneau, I was invited to join them at the governor's mansion for a party. Aunt Belle gave me a beautiful aquamarine ring so I would have some jewelry to wear. Governor Greuning and his lovely wife would greet us at the door of the mansion. They would welcome us with great hospitality, lead us to the food, offer hors d'oeuvres, wind up the victrola, and retire upstairs to their bedroom to read while the sailors and I danced and ate. At the end of the evening (around 10:00), they would appear to say goodbye to their guests and tell us, "It was a pleasure to be with you."

My cousin, Bob Goldstein, and some of his drunken friends called me one night at the governor's mansion to embarrass me. They thought Aunt Belle and the other older ladies I was staying with were too haughty, and they wanted me to have more fun with their friends rather than party with the white-suited sailors.

Belle represented Alaska at the American Legion convention in Paris and on other Chamber of Commerce trips. On Alaska's bi-centennial, Aunt Belle was honored by the city of Juneau with "Belle Simpson Day."

Annabelle Simpson

Belle's children were Annabelle and Robert. They both graduated from Stanford. I loved and admired them both. Robert became a doctor and settled in Seattle. He and his first wife, Bess, had four boys. One of them, Peter, went to the London School of Economics and married an Italian woman. They live in Trento, Italy, and have two sons. With Norman and the children we met them in Milan. My friend Kay and I met their son Richard in Verona. Richard has visited us often in Lafayette.

Annabelle was a beautiful model and a newspaper reporter. She was tall and freckled-faced, with brown curly hair and the most wonderful, sparkling smile. She sat on the left of Tom Dewey in Juneau when he ran for president of the United States. I modeled my young life after Annabelle. She was a student body officer at Stanford and a leader in the fight against sororities (I didn't believe in them either). She worked as a reporter for the *Chronicle*, traveled the world, and met the most important people. Shetold me to request a private room at Stanford. I probably wanted to go to Stanford because of her. I loved her. She introduced me to a lovely South African couple from *Reuters News* when I was alone in London.

Annabelle was married twice, once out of Stanford and once to a prominent judge in Anchorage. She was still very beautiful when I listened to her ideas at my Aunt Carol's home one Thanksgiving. I decided I didn't relate to her values at all. While I was in college, Annabelle had a nervous breakdown in Rome. Robert flew to Europe to bring her home. I knew nothing about it at the time. My mother told me when I got home to Weiser after my graduation.

I last saw Annabelle when she called me from the bus station in Pleasant Hill, California, around 2010. I picked her up. She was changed. She looked old and wasted and was shaking nervously. She stayed with us for four days, but she wouldn't come out of the bedroom even to eat. She ate the candy bars she carried with her. Finally, Norman decided she had to move on. She died in a rest home in Seattle around the age of forty-five. Her mother, Belle, died in Seattle at the age of one hundred and one.

Within the last twenty years, Alaska has claimed more of my relatives: Robert's two sons, Belle's grandsons, who were in their twenties. Their small plane crashed in the mountains while they were photographing mountain goats. One of the bodies has never been found.

Mollie and Hyman Greenblatt Seattle 1910

Mollie Greenblatt

MOLLIE GOLDSTEIN WAS MY GRANDMOTHER. She was born in Winnipeg, Manitoba, in 1880. Records there showed she was the oldest living person born in Winnipeg before she died at one hundred and one years in San Francisco in 1980. She went to school at the Catholic convent with her sisters, Flora, Esther, Minnie, and Belle. It was the only school in Juneau at that time. Mollie studied French and music. The girls were excused from religious training by the nuns because they were Jewish. Snow often piled above the fences and over the windows as Mollie and her sisters walked to the convent. She was clad in high rubber gumboots that came above her knees. She made her own path, her boots filling with snow—she recalled emptying one boot while the other would fill with snow. Mollie was married at sixteen to Hyman Greenblatt in 1896. He was older. It was an arranged marriage, as was common in that day. Mollie, her curly hair drawn back, towers above Hyman in old daguerreotypes. Hyman is shown in his striped suit with his watch chain hanging below.

Hyman homesteaded at Port Townsend, Washington. He thought it would become the biggest city on the West Coast. Homestead documents signed by President Benjamin Harrison in 1891 and President McKinley in 1898 testify to Hyman's faith in that city. Port Townsend was filled with beautiful Victorian mansions. Unfortunately, Great Northern Railway, the railroad to the West, ran out of money in Seattle in 1884.

When Seattle became the biggest city on the West Coast instead of Port Townsend, Mollie and Hyman moved there. They opened a jewelry store at 620 Jackson Street near the future Japanese section of town. Mollie worked in the store alongside Hyman. Their home was on Capitol Hill. Hyman was struck by a horse and buggy during the children's adolescence. All I ever heard was that after that, "he was never the same." Personal matters were never discussed with me, as I was always considered "the baby." I would guess Hyman was bedridden for a while before he died.

Mollie was left with two beautiful daughters and one son. She sold the jewelry store and supported her family by collecting rents from tenants in her small apartment houses in downtown Seattle; I sometimes went with her. When Ruby married Ed Sugarman, she was persuaded to move to San Francisco. She left many friends. But many of her friends later moved to the San Francisco Bay Area.

Mollie Greenblatt   date unknown

Mollie's family grew up in a large, wooden house at 523 14th Avenue North on Capitol Hill. It was a hill of mansions leading to Volunteer Park. The Greenblatt house was near the end on a narrow tree-lined street. A walk from the cement sidewalk led past the dogwood tree up the steps to the front porch. In the entry hall was the shiny, black, carved Chinese table with the turtle—it sits in our San Francisco apartment now. (It may possibly be German, as I saw similar furniture in Cecilienhof in Potsdam, Germany.) On top of the table sat the bright azure blue cloisonné vase with the pink hydrangeas. It is today a lamp on the same black table in our San Francisco apartment. On the top of the railing of the large, double staircase sat the pot iron cupid pointing upward to the landing. It is now in my living room as the base of another old-fashioned lamp. On the first landing at the top of the back staircase was a victrola with a flower-shaped speaker. Beneath the victrola was the cabinet that held the scratchy 78-rpm opera records. That cabinet is now in Bruce's den.

The back staircase led down to a small room with a bench on which to talk on the black handheld phone. You would dial a number, and a live operator would answer and connect you. You would listen by way of the separate, black-cord-connected receiver.

In front of the living room fireplace was the davenport.

The front bay window seat was where I used to sit to watch the rain. The floors were covered with red-and blue-patterned oriental rugs. Glass doors led to the dining room, and behind the dining room was a glass-enclosed sun porch for sewing and other activities. The kitchen was small, with a wood burning stove. The iceman came every week to deliver a big block of ice to the icebox on the back porch. In the upstairs hall was a glass-enclosed bookcase. A large double room extended the full length of the front of the house. The white tile bathroom with the lion-footed tub was entered from this bedroom and the hall. On the back side of the hall were two bedrooms, one for Mollie and Hyman and one for Ruby. Off both of these bedrooms were screened-in sleeping porches. The staircase turned and continued to the attic, which was used for storage.

The house was the stopping-off place for Mollie's large Alaskan family. Relatives were often at the dinner table while on their journeys to California and back. Mollie enjoyed all her visitors, and they probably enjoyed the free stay. They brought her canned salmon from Alaska. The maids were instructed on the proper service, and help was always available.

Ruby

Mollie's oldest daughter, my Aunt Ruby, played the violin. A tall, beautiful woman, she was engaged to a man named Max Cohn. Right after the engagement party, he died of pneumonia. She gave up the violin and went to work for Washington State. Weekends she would lie on the davenport in front of the fireplace and listen to classical music. Every Saturday morning, we heard the Metropolitan Opera matinee together.

Ruby married twice, once to a man from New York and next to Ed Sugarman, a bacteriologist in

Ruby and Ed in San Francisco during my summer vacations. On summer Sundays, we went to Stern Grove. Aunt Ruby gave a party for me in her ballroom and saw that I met people from San Francisco. She was responsible for my going to Camp Talawonga with her friend's daughters one special summer.

Ed had two derelict sons who treated her rudely. Ruby and Ed lived in a beautiful home in Pacific Heights that belonged to Ed's deceased wife. After Ed died, his daughter-in-law and two sons gave my aunt one month to move out so they could sell it. Apartments were scarce in San Francisco. She had to move in with Mollie in a one-room apartment and sleep in a rollaway bed until Mollie could find an apartment with two bedrooms. She inherited Ed's bacteriology lab at 450 Sutter Street. It was encumbered with debt. She had to go to work every day at Galileo High School to pay off his debts.

Aunt Ruby was a traveler. She went around the world with a friend who was called home during the trip because of her daughter's death. Ruby continued alone to Kathmandu, Nepal. It was just opening to tourists and didn't even have electricity: no electric lights, and the irons had to be heated over a fire. She told of flying there in a small plane, alone, with unchained cages of squawking birds rolling around in front and unfettered suitcases rolling around behind her. She told me she was sitting in between them crunched up when the plane lost altitude over the mountains, and she wondered, "What am I doing here?" She told of meeting Leontine Price in her hotel in Vienna. She took my mother to Hong Kong and Japan. That was the only time my mother traveled abroad.

Ruby was a brave and interesting woman and an outstanding aunt. She loved Norman and was so supportive of me. I felt I could really talk to her. She took care of her mother until Mollie died at the age of one hundred and one.

Robert

Mollie's son, Robert Greenblatt, left home early. He married Vera while Mollie and I were in Alaska. Vera was a wonderful daughter-in-law to Mollie. Robert and Vera both died in the 1950s.

My Mother's Life

Belle Greenblatt 1930

Belle

M Y MOTHER, BELLE, HAD MANY friends and beaus. She graduated from the University of Washington with a degree in education. In order to be certified she had to move to a small town to teach. Hyman, her father, forbid her to go because, "nice girls don't leave home." Her cutest boyfriend, she recalled later, "was always at our house, and he was very poor." Belle had many friends from college, including Frieda and Florence—they were close all her life.

Mama spoke of a young woman two years ahead of her in college. "She was so beautiful. She danced a mean Charleston, she was a communist, she married a millionaire." I think my mother felt threatened by this lovely woman. Her daughter later became my college roommate. I spent many happy hours at her home. My mother was deathly afraid of the Bolsheviks and the IWW. She was very conservative and did what she was told. She later worried that I would develop liberal ideas. I did!

Joe Eder

MY FATHER, JOSEPH EDER, CAME to Seattle from Milwaukee to visit his cousins, Bessie Asia and Sara Miller. They were Mollie's friends. Joe was an exotic, intelligent stranger, well-educated and wealthy. Short, stocky, and balding, with steel rimmed glasses, he had a master's degree in classics and read ancient Greek. He could quote the *Iliad*, the *Odyssey* and the *Aeneid* by heart.

He was born in Hungary and came to Milwaukee in 1892. He was a member of the first graduating class of the University of Wisconsin law school in 1907. He practiced law from 1907 until 1917. He then formed the Eder Flag Manufacturing Company. He owned gas stations in both Illinois and Wisconsin. He loved all sports, especially golf and swimming. He regaled the Greenblatt family with stories of his impressive education and wealth. When Joe came to Seattle, he was close to Mollie's age and twenty-four years older than my mother.

Belle enjoyed many boyfriends and probably would have married one of them. Mollie had other ideas. Joe gave Ruby, Belle, and Mollie beautiful presents, including silver dressing-table sets. He regaled the family with stories of great riches in Milwaukee.

Hyman was dead, and it was decided that Belle should marry Joe. The ring was a two-carat square-cut diamond. Very few people could afford such a diamond in the Depression. My mother was beautiful in her long, lace wedding dress, with Ruby as her maid of honor. Neither of them smiled. It was 1931, the beginning of the worldwide Depression.

Joseph Eder 1933

Belle Greenblatt 1932

Milwaukee

My mother and father took the train to Milwaukee, where they were met by all my father's relatives. There was his brother Morris and his wife Olga, Henry, Sam, etc. I remember my sweet Aunt Olga. She was from Hungary, her slip was always showing, she had tight curly hair, she was loud and always nervous. She and Uncle Morris had four children. I don't believe either of them had an education. Olga was very different in refinement from my mother. Morris, Olga, her four children, and my father and mother went everywhere together, because the brothers had only one car. Joe would often walk, no matter how far. He was a person with no concept of time. Since he was a wanderer, he must have left my mother waiting for hours alone. My mother was very unhappy.

The Depression took its toll. My mother's favorite sister-in-law, Bea, worked on the *Settlement Cookbook*. She had one son, Doctor Howard Eder. Another brother's wife hanged herself leaving behind four children. Sissy, the oldest, went to Uncle John in New York, Suzy blended in with Olga's four children; Philip went to Seattle to live with Aunt Bessie; Jim was adopted as a baby by a distant aunt.

My father's youngest brother, John, was a New York lawyer who graduated from Harvard. He had married a socialite, Ann, who never came back to see the family in Milwaukee. He later became my favorite uncle. I met many new cousins in his law office at 525 5th Avenue when I was young.

I was born in 1933 during the worldwide Depression. The racist National Socialist Party of Germany elected Adolf Hitler chancellor. Nobody knew about the Holocaust, except for vague news of an enormous rally in Madison Square Garden in New York, where Rabbi Stephen S. Wise alerted the Jewish community to the atrocities.

Milwaukee had a branch of the Bund. My father argued with the family for appeasement and his pacifist ideals. Whatever side you were on, Joe was on the distaff side,. He lectured on and on. He would talk for hours about the ancient Greeks, Dostoevsky, and other boring classical topics.

My mother and father's first home was the upstairs of a duplex. My mother bought beautiful furniture. (The davenport in our bedroom, the two dining room settees, as well as the silverware set, were what was left from that home.)

My grandmother came by train to Milwaukee. My mother and I went back with her to Seattle. I rarely saw my father. Once he drove a car Mollie bought in the east to Seattle for her. Life in Milwaukee was over. As my grandmother scrubbed me in the white clawfoot tub, I learned about the divorce. I was two years old.

Seattle

My mother and I moved into the large front room in Mollie's home on Capitol Hill. I went to school in Seattle. I remember Temple de Hirsch and snow sledding down Capitol Hill. Aunt Ruby walked me to Volunteer Park every Saturday morning to see the Lone Ranger movies in the Seattle Art Museum. Mama worked as a dress sales woman. Mollie took care of me. I remember cans of Campbell's Soup that she opened in the kitchen when I came home from school for my lunch break. I took piano lessons. I was a lonely child, and my mother was divorced.

I remember driving around the neighborhoods in Seattle with my sad, divorced mother and admiring all the beautiful homes and lovely gardens in places like Magnolia Bluff. My mother had a daughter, but she didn't have a home. She longed for a home of her own.

Occasionally my father would take the train from Milwaukee to Seattle to see me. It was a long trip. He would buy me presents, a tricycle, a puppy, or sweaters from I. Magnin. His visits were very emotional for me. I cried when I was with him and when he left.

My cousin Phil Eder lived with my Aunt Bessie in an apartment down Capitol Hill. He must have been lonely too. He often came to see me. He was just a little bit older than me. When I visited Seattle, he took me to the beach.

German Jews began arriving in Seattle from the Orient. My family met them at the boats and welcomed them to their home. I remember a tall, teenaged boy in spats standing on our front porch. He was handsome and very sad. In 1939 Germany marched into Poland, and on December 7, 1941, Japan bombed Pearl Harbor. The Japanese in Seattle were swiftly moved to internment camps in the desert. I was a child, and I knew nothing about it— nobody discussed it with me. On December 8th, 1941, President Franklin D. Roosevelt asked Congress to declare war.

Sam Emrich

I WAS SEVEN YEARS OLD WHEN Sam Emrich came to Seattle to buy furniture for the Globe Furniture Company of Weiser, Idaho. He was a self-made man with only a third-grade education. He started with nothing and built a furniture store that serviced the entire surrounding area of his small town. He was short and barrel-chested, with straight black hair. He had a sparkle in his eyes and a charm that drew you to him. He also bragged about being wealthy.

His father had died. He, his mother, brother, and three sisters were brought to New

Plymouth, Idaho, from Atlanta, Georgia, by an uncle, Herman Haas. The family spoke with a soft southern accent.

Sam built up a big business in Weiser with the Globe Furniture Store and gave his three sisters and his brother jobs. The family lived together in a white gabled home. Sam, then in his forties, escorted his mother everywhere until she died.

Stella, my college roommate's aunt, was his cousin. She lived in the brick apartment house next door to Mollie's home. Stella introduced Sam to Belle. Sam wanted to take Belle to Vancouver. I cried so hard they finally took me along. Later, I drove with my mother to visit Weiser. On the drive, I reached out the widow to catch one of the round, floating tumbleweeds, and the sharp stickers tore at my hand. It was an omen of my future life in Weiser, both beautiful and hurtful.

When my mother decided to marry Sam, I was eight years old. I was sad about leaving Seattle. I told my mother I would never see my few friends again. She told me they would turn up. They did, at Stanford, but there they became merely acquaintances.

Sam's sister, Rita, gave a reception in our honor. My luggage had been lost on the train, and I had to buy a dress. The only clothing store in Weiser had little to offer. They bought me a flowery dress that was too young for me, and I looked terrible. I was also fat, and I was embarrassed. I wore that dress for years.

Aunt Rita was very sweet, but too inquisitive for my mother. We moved into a small, white clapboard house between Sam's family home and the Nazarene Church on West Idaho Street. My mother drew the shades for privacy. I was in the middle of the third grade. They didn't have half semesters in Weiser, so I was put ahead to the fourth grade.

That fall Aunt Rita brought her niece Eloise from Portland to live with her next door. Eloise was mentally challenged and was having a hard time in Portland, where she lived with her family, since there were no facilities for handicapped there. She was two years older than me. She was put in my grade in school. I had to walk to school with Eloise every day. I could not go anywhere without her. I watched the children across the street walk together, but I was stuck.

TRAVELS WITH AN ARTIST

When I asked to take a friend with us to a movie in a nearby town, I can still hear Uncle Sam saying, "Why should I take some stranger's child to the movies when my sister's child sits home." One day a friend said to me, "Let's ditch Eloise." Aunt Rita heard about it and gave me hell. I wanted Aunt Rita's approval so badly.

I had a hard time making friends, because I was young and shy, and Eloise had to come with me every place I went. Children don't understand. Uncle Sam favored Eloise and used to kiss her in the furniture store right in front of me. If my mother and Sam had a fight, Uncle Sam drove Eloise to school without me.

I always called him Uncle Sam. Everybody in Weiser did. I think that really bothered him. He wanted to adopt me but my father, Joe, wouldn't sign the papers. I couldn't call him father. I had a father, even though he wasn't around. My last name was Eder. I went by the name Emrich because the kids at school always asked me, "Why is your name different from your families?"

Uncle Sam paid for me to go to Stanford. He was very good to me. I always tried to please and impress him. I never felt I did. He always made me feel guilty. My name on my diploma from Stanford is Emrich, but my passport had to be notarized Eder-Emrich. It was really upsetting. I had no problem later changing my name to Licht.

During the Second World War, Uncle Sam bought a black seven-passenger Packard. There was a shortage of cars, and that large car was what you called a lemon. It looked like a hearse. I was so embarrassed by it, I would ride on the floor in the back seat, scooched way down over the closed jump seats. I remember once driving to Seattle with my friend Claire. We strung Japanese origami paper birds out of the windows. It was the only fun I ever had in that car.

Our other car was a Cadillac. However, I never learned to drive until after I graduated from college. Weiser was very poor. My folks and I were conscious of our Jewishness, and I was always worried about being called a "rich Jew."

My mother wanted a piano so I could resume my lessons. She also wanted a home for privacy away from Aunt Rita and the church. She lived in a small, old home with a wealthy man. She and Uncle Sam argued about it constantly. She became head of the Weiser Red Cross during the war. The main project was the knitting of gray sweaters for the fighting troops. She joined a bridge club and rose to be statewide president of the PTA. She later started the Weiser Historical Museum, collecting old costumes, furniture, documents, etc. from the farm homes around. She was able to purchase magnificent hand-carved antiques for herself and the museum.

In old-fashioned costumes, she was the MC for the first fiddler's festival parade, the tiny hillbilly get-together in August that later became the famous Fiddler's Festival. It turned into an annual event attracting international fiddlers like Mark O'Connor and others. She owned the "put-put," a tiny, open, gas-run car that is now in the Weiser Historical Museum. When our children, David, Bruce, and Lisa, were young, they drove the "put-put", dressed in old-fashioned costumes in the parade when they visited Weiser.

Belle and Sam Emrich 1948

The Globe Furniture Company

The furniture store grew to encompass an entire block. Slow Uncle Bert would come down around eleven o'clock in the rain, soaking the davenports with his wet raincoat as he sat and emptied his pipe on the damp cement floor. Uncle Sam used to call him "Sugar Boy," but Bert never felt he was demeaned. He always drew his salary, as did Sam's three sisters. Aunt Rita brought a pleuritic husband home from New York as a bookkeeper. Uncle Sam called him "Napoleon"—I guess he endured it, as it came with a job.

The store provided menial jobs for many of the poor local people. The furniture was cheap and sold on credit. Cheesy plaid davenports, second-hand stoves, Formica tables, gaudy lamps, and other pieces were of questionable style. My mother bought better furniture for her home, as she was trained to know the difference. One snowy midnight in January, the store burned to the ground. It was rebuilt.

Every evening, Uncle Sam went to the post office for his mail. My mother always wanted me to go with him. He used to make remarks that made me very uncomfortable. He would tell me, "Every other girl your age is married, why aren't you?" and, "No one will marry you, because your uncle owns a bar." I had no one in mind to marry. Some of his worst comments were, "Why can't you be useful like every other girl your age. You can't even serve a cup of coffee without spilling it." and, "You should be a waitress so you could learn to serve a cup of coffee," I tried to ignore him, as I knew I was going to college. He upset me internally, and I always felt uneasy.

Every Sunday, we drove to Baker, Oregon, a desolate, dreary drive of two hours over boring landscape. Uncle Sam had set up his brother-in-law, my Uncle Julien, in a branch of the Globe Furniture Company there. I read poetry and books in the car and the Baker store. Sometimes Uncle Sam was so impatient to leave Weiser that I hardly had time to grab a book. We visited his sister, Aunt Elsie, and Uncle Julien. Berta, their daughter, was five years younger and very popular. I never saw her until we met each other years later in California and became close friends. Eloise still lived in Weiser. I sometimes saw my friend, Claire.

Mrs. Whittemore

Certain teachers enriched my life. My English teacher, Mrs. Whittemore, was so conscientious that when I wrote my entrance exam, I was able to skip English 1, "bonehead English," at Stanford. An elegant, refined woman, she lived as a recluse with her daughter, Jean, in an old gabled house on a main street. We never visited her there. She invited me back to her classroom to talk to her students about my trip to Europe two years after I graduated from college. On her classroom wall there was a photo of the nearby mountain, Old Indian Head, and below it was my first published poem, "Ode to Old Indian Head."

Ford Smith

Ford Smith taught music at Weiser High School. A staunch Mormon, as was most of the town, he attended Mutual every week. This handsome, dark-haired man ran the high school band. We marched around the football field at 7:00 a.m. before school started each day, even when it rained. Our uniforms consisted of gray pants, maroon jackets with gold braid and buttons, and commando hats. We were so proud.

We followed every parade from Payette to Nampa. The band marched before the football games on Friday nights and on the Fourth of July. First came the white-booted, high-hatted, short-skirted majorettes twirling batons, then the antique cars, with the mayors and other dignities tossing out candy. Then came the small floats, if there were any. The band marched behind the cowboys riding on their decorated horses. We were instructed not to miss a step. We had to clean the horse manure off our brown and white saddle shoes after each parade.

I played the alto saxophone. "Stars and Stripes Forever" was our song. If the footing and the notes couldn't come together, I only pretended to hit the keys. No one ever knew. We traveled as far as Idaho Falls and places in between for band contests. Little Gene carried my heavy sax for me. I felt light and lucky. Families stood on the sidewalks and cheered. Football was the way of small-town life.

When a traveling company of the Ballet Russes de Monte Carlo, *Carmen*, or *La Traviata* came to Boise, Ford would load us all into the little, yellow school bus and take us there to see it. We felt we never missed a thing.

Clark Hamilton

CLARK HAMILTON'S GENERAL STORE STOOD at an angle on the confluence of State and Main Street, across from the post office on the edge of downtown. It was a heated haven from our freezing winter walk. Shovels, food, and ironing boards were among his stock. The pungent aroma of overripe fruit, the sweet smell of wood chips, and the acrid smell of musk filled the shop. During our Christmas vacation in 1943, my friend Judy and I strolled inside. We were two little girls with nothing to do. We wandered through the store, touching the merchandise and sniffing the produce.

We were ten years old. Clark, the lone proprietor, seemed a very old man to us. He must have been around forty. Tall and thin, he was a Mark Twain lookalike, with center-parted gray hair, mustache, and round steel-rimmed glasses. He was tieless that day. He was wearing a gray woolen vest from which dangled a large round silver watch on a golden chain over an open buttoned-down striped cotton shirt with rolled up sleeves. A studious scholar, he lived quietly with his piano-playing wife in a brown wooden house up the street from his store. He was not a family friend. He spent much of his time alone with his books.

"Let's steal something!"

"OK"

We stole three small oranges.

"Hey you! Stop!" Clark shouted furiously. We ran.

Bending his elbow and waving his clenched fist high in the air, Clark sped out of the warm, wooden warehouse leaving the front door wide open. The snowplow had just been through. The dirty white snow was piled high on the curbs. He chased us all the way down the wet, carless street to the middle of town. No one was around. He reached out and caught us by our collars. We were scared. As we shivered and sweated in the frigid air under our heavy woolen coats, he glowered at our guilty red faces. He quickly retrieved the three small, smashed, sticky oranges from our trembling hands and admonished:

"I'll call the police!" (He didn't.)

and even worse,

"I'll tell your parents!" (He didn't.)

We cowed before him, extremely embarrassed and remorseful.

I never stole anything again in my life!

I grew up in Weiser. I rode out of town with my folks to collect rent from poor tenants on my stepfather's unkempt ranch. It was on the side of the cliff, high above the Snake River. The tenants loaded us up with fresh vegetables. I rode Spot, our glass-eyed horse and fed him many, many carrots.

I swam in the public pool and became a hesitant lifeguard. I wrote the high school column for Harry Nelson's newspaper, the *Weiser Signal*, and ushered at the local movie house, the Star Theater. One of my poems was published in a state magazine entitled, "Surprising Idaho." I played the alto saxophone in the high school band as it traveled all over the state.

We skated on frozen ponds in winter and played terrible tennis in the summer. I read every classic book in the small, storefront library, listened to lovesick, lonely, cowboy songs and dreamed of someday traveling very far from home.

Clark later became a state senator and wrote me a beautiful recommendation to Stanford.

Uncle Sam, my mother, and me

Cattle drive in Weiser, Idaho 1949

I T WAS THE LATE 1940S, a long way from the cities and the small towns. Fat little Gene, the local boy who carried my heavy saxophone on high school band trips, invited me to come with him on a cattle drive. I rode a horse beside him. Little Gene's family owned most of the cattle. He lived on a disheveled Idaho farm with pigs, chickens, bashed brown buckets, and barefoot brothers and sisters dressed in filthy, ill-fitting clothes.

The drive started at dawn. The horses had to be hitched, the corrals had to be opened, and a ham-and-eggs breakfast was served in the makeshift wooden cookhouse. For some of the men, breakfast was accompanied by whiskey from their private flasks.

The wide, dusty, road was flat, unpaved, pocked with tire tracks, and dried from the winter's rain. Rolling, gossamer, tumbleweeds floated like fairies over short golden grass and occasional wildflowers, covering calm countryside that extended for miles.

A luminous haze hung about the top of distant Old Indian Head Mountain. Its lower level of grayish, green pine trees dancing slowly in the breeze seemed to be sizzling side feathers on the back of the cloak of the bronzed old man sleeping soundly beneath the sky.

You didn't have to speak English to drive cattle in the country. All you had to do was go, "Haaaaaaaaa," or "Waaaaaaaaah," as loud and as harsh as you could, over and over, as the bovines slowly moved along. The cows rode languidly in rows of five or six, with a lazy, lanky cowboy ambling his horse on the side of every ten rows. Sometimes the men would whip, sometimes they would push, sometimes they would kick to keep the cows moving. The dirty, dusty men rode slowly to the trains or the slaughterhouses, thinking vacant thoughts. They swayed to the moo of the cows, the bark of the dogs, and the arcing of the birds, as if to slow, liturgical music.

Each cow had the brand of its owner burned on its rear, an obsolete, antiquated tradition. In 1949 no one cared about cruelty to animals. Today the cattle are branded with permanent, colorful oil sticks painted on the back of their hides.

Dentists were expensive and hard to find. Crooked teeth were yellowed from tobacco. Some of the men were missing one or two or even more. Some of them chain smoked. Some had cigarettes hanging from their mouths unlit. Poorly paid, poorly housed, wizened, wrinkled, bored, and slouched, these illiterate men would go from cattle drive to cattle drive, drifting slowly around the country.

The restless, itinerant men often came from distant locations, riding the tops of the peeling, painted, wooden freight trains that traversed the West at that time. Occasionally one of them carried a battered old radio to listen to mournful cowboy tunes like "Old Buttermilk Sky" or "Red River Valley." The jokes were poor, the language was crude and completely without syntax. Hillbilly English was the norm. As the sun beat down in the heavy heat of noon, some of the shirtless men became sunburnt, roasting redly beneath their flattened cowboy hats. Typically, they had ridden without a break since dawn.

Sometimes guests, a foreign student from Stanford or some other Ivy League school wanting to understand the United States, would try their hand at cattle driving for a day. One day was enough! The cattle drive was the underbelly of the country, and people during the forties and fifties all ate beef!

Payday was Saturday. The exhausted men dragged straight to the bars in the closest small town, to spend their meager bounty on whiskey and lonely, available women. Sunday was spent sleeping off their drunken brawls. If they heard of a rodeo in one of the surrounding tiny towns, they would try their hand at lassoing and bronco busting. That was the big excitement of the week.

Did the wars and progress take these men, viral and uneducated? Were they killed? Did they return? Did some go to college on the GI Bill?

Where are the cattle drives now?

Claire

CLAIRE WAS MY BEST FRIEND. She lived two hours away in Baker, Oregon. She was a jubilant, freckle-faced, dark, curly haired girl with a radiant smile and personality. We really clicked. Her beautiful mother Marion, was a devoted Mormon, a former hairdresser, and the sister of the famous swimsuit designer, Rose Marie Reid. Her Jewish father, Sanford, owned the Baker Department Store. Claire had three little brothers and a skunk (de-skunked, of course) that was a miserable creature.

Sanford had six old brothers with names like Gerson and Hans. He had brought them over from Germany. They worked in his department store. All were short, bald, and spoke with a barely understandable German accent. The bachelor brothers lived together frugally in a small upstairs apartment over the store in downtown Baker.

When Claire was in high school, one of the old brothers died and left her some money. She immediately bought a little turquoise convertible and drove it to Weiser to show it to me. It was something I couldn't have imagined.

I slept over some weekends with her in Baker. Once, when I went with her to Sunday school at the Mormon Church, I remember hearing it said that, "Jews were the lost tribes of Israel." Knowing little of Judaism, even less of Mormonism, I never went back. Weiser was a Mormon community, and most of the kids went to Mutual meetings on Wednesday nights. Claire was half Jewish and half Mormon. Her Mormonism took precedent.

Claire and I were mischievous. One Sunday we opened all the windows in my bedroom next to the Nazarene Church and blasted out all the radios during their service. We were appropriately punished. We never did that again.

Claire asked me to go to Annie Wright Seminary with her. It was a private college preparatory high school in Tacoma. My cousin Anabelle had gone there before she went to Stanford. I wanted to go so badly. We planned to room together and to be roommates at Stanford later on. Mama said, "No, you can have your choice, Annie Wright or Stanford." I thought she was unreasonable. I begged her, "Mama, if I don't go to Annie Wright, I'll never get in to Stanford."

Claire went to Annie Wright alone. Annie Wright wouldn't let her apply to Stanford. She had had too much fun, and her grades fell. She went to Finch College in New York and later transferred to UCLA. I was accepted to Stanford from Weiser High School.

Idaho Judaism

I knew I was Jewish. Uncle Sam was the head of the United Jewish Appeal in Weiser. He gave $1,000 every year and collected money from the five other Jewish families in town. My mother had a Sunday school in our basement. She sent for workbooks for the children of the five Jewish families. None of us children liked the Sunday school. I had to stay out of school on the Jewish holidays while our family spent the day visiting with the other Jewish families. I was dejected to miss the Saturday football games.

There were two temples in Boise. The reform temple was Congregation Ahavath Beth Israel. Its 1896 building was the oldest synagogue building in continuous use west of the Mississippi River. It was dedicated in 1895 with 25 Jewish families. The newer synagogue was conservative. My mother belonged to both. She felt more at home in the reform temple. The reform temple had only eleven members at the end of the 1940s. One of the congregants served as the reader. One of the original members, a haberdasher, founded the temple and later became mayor of Boise, then governor of Idaho. He was the first Jewish governor in the United States. I dated his grandson all through my time at Stanford and after I graduated.

A charming young Jewish man from Boise came to Weiser with records of *La Boheme*. I was in college and completely enthralled. *Che Gelida Manina* will always remind me of him. He explained the opera to me and made it come alive. He was a singer, and he probably ended up as a cantor. He left me his *Boheme* records. My parents worried that I liked him too much, and they felt his family was not social enough for them. Uncle Sam made me return the album. I caught my fingers in the car door. I cried and cried. Their ideas were so wrong!

Stanford and Beyond

NOTHING PREPARED ME FOR THE truly astounding plethora of ideas at Stanford when I entered in 1950. I chose Stanford because of its lack of sororities, a system that I felt discriminated against the unchosen person's life. I wanted to be a newspaper reporter and travel all over the world. I was full of anticipation, awaiting my steamer trunk containing the hat and gloves that every proper Stanford student had to wear from time to time.

I wanted to take every class offered. "Too many classes," said my advisor as he steered me into freshman English, Spanish 1, and political science. Skipping "bonehead" English with my essay on driving cattle in Idaho was a big mistake. I didn't know how to study. I was totally ignorant of writing a college term paper. I felt I aced my first freshman quarter with a C. My mother told me, "That was a very good start." I felt relieved.

My first dorm room was private, on the second floor over the front door of Roble Hall. My cousin, Annabelle, advised me to request it. It was a great idea. My friends often gathered in my room. Looking out the window, seeing the comings and goings, was distracting to my studies. I dated all the time.

Naivete was my middle name. Stanford changed me. I was shocked at my ignorance. Some of the conservative ideals of my family gave me great guilt. I was introduced to a whole new set of values that I try to hold on to today.

It was the time of Senator Joe McCarthy, the Hollywood Seven, the Rosenberg trial, and the communist scare. Those things were unheard of in Idaho, where the only newspapers,

The Oregonian and *The Idaho Statesman*, carried very little news that wasn't local. I spent spare time on campus with my friends, listening to the McCarthy hearings on small black-and-white televisions. I was made aware of Roy Cohn and the injustice of the loyalty oath. That requirement made people swear they had never attended a meeting or been a member of the Communist Party. In order to keep their faculty positions, professors were required to sign it at Cal and other state schools. Producers and actors like Robert Taylor, Ronald Reagan, John Wayne, and Walt Disney named names to the House Un-American Activities Committee. My Los Angeles friends knew people in the movies who were barred from working. These were issues I knew nothing about. I realized that developing a social conscience was of great value for me.

Some people refused to sign the oath out of sympathy for friends, or purely because they disapproved of being coerced. It was rumored that students sat in classes and reported professors who showed signs of disloyalty. This oath hurt people and brought on fear and conformity. Senator McCarthy spoke in San Mateo during my freshman year. Many Stanford students went to hear him. My friends and I heard Frank Lloyd Wright that night instead. We said, "Two men spoke around Stanford. One was Wright and the other was wrong." (We knew very little about Wright at that time.)

My friends and I passed petitions against the loyalty oath, but many Stanford students refused to sign. People were scared. The husband of my cousin Aileen Ann was a physics professor at San Francisco State. He did not sign. He lost his professorship and his lovely San Francisco home. Before Aline Ann died, I asked her, "Are you really a communist?" She told me she was a communist. That didn't make any difference to me. It was her choice. My wealthy great-uncle Charlie, her grandfather, who had sent her to Stanford after her parents died, left her only one dollar in his will. That was not right.

Camel cigarettes were handed out to students in small packets at the entrance to campuses. It seemed grown-up to smoke. I didn't care for smoking, and couldn't afford it.

TRAVELS WITH AN ARTIST

I did write a jingle for the Lucky Strike college contest that won me twenty-five dollars. It was more money than my bookstore job paid me, where I worked before my classes started.

I worked on the *Stanford Daily*. I thought newspaper work would be my career, and it was my favorite job on campus. I started out as a reporter and rose to be a copy writer. It was a privilege to interview bright people who were involved with world-changing ideas. I loved the excitement, the deadlines, the *Daily* parties, and my byline when I had an interview or story of interest.

I interviewed Alain Enthoven, who later became a professor in the Stanford Graduate School of Business. He was the head of the Symphony Forum. He invited me to go with him and another couple to meetings in the San Francisco Opera House every other week. We signed a scroll to Pierre Monteaux, the conductor of the symphony at the time. We enjoyed lunch, and on the campus we distributed leftover tickets to the Thursday student nights at the symphony. My friend Joan drove us into the city. When I offered to pay for the gas, she said, "Oh, I just charge it. Then nobody has to pay for it." We always stopped by the old Museum of Modern Art on the way. This was my first real introduction to classical music. One of my boyfriends invited me out for a hamburger one night and asked me what I thought of Mahler. I was from Idaho. I had never heard of Mahler!

I had to resign the *Daily* during my junior year to bring up my grade point average. I really missed it. Stanford was a banquet. I wanted to take every class, from Russian literature to poetry, political science, existentialism, and music. I probably overextended myself because Stanford offered so much. My best friends, and later my roommates, shared the same interests: foreign students, world affairs, and loading up on classes. We belonged to the Cosmopolitan Club, a weekly meeting club for foreign students. My friends had great depth. On Fridays, when most students went to drink beer at Rosotti's, the local drinking spot, we entertained young patients at the Stanford Con (convalescent) Home. The boys in our crowd had a band, and the girls danced and visited with the children.

Some of the young college boys were drafted from school for the terrible Korean War. My roommate MeraLee's fiancé, Leonard, was one of them.

Incidentally, I studied. School was hard but worth it.

MeraLee

MeraLee was one of my sophomore and junior class roommates. We first met at the Stanford post office thinking, *Is she or isn't she Jewish?* She came from Chicago, where she had gone to the University of Chicago High School. She had many credits from there. She was younger than me, petite and pretty with dark brown hair and a friendly, bubbling personality. She was an only child, and her mother, Sylvia, visited her often and always gave her a party or took the three of us to dinner. Sylvia was very inclusive and supportive of our friendship. MeraLee was so clever. She influenced my love of art and colorful modern design. Her sweaters were monogramed.

I traded clothes sometimes with my other roommate, since we both loved wearing black t-shirts, short skirts, and sandals. My mother bought all my clothes for me before I entered. I never learned to shop. One of my dates felt my sweater and asked if it was cashmere—it wasn't. Clothes were never important to me at college. I had no trouble keeping up. I cut my hair by putting a bowl over my head and trimming. I wore no jewelry or makeup. When you are young, you always look good.

MeraLee and I went together to big game during our freshman year. We each didn't accept the dates we were offered. Meralee found her boyfriend, Leonard, right after Christmas vacation her freshman year. She dated him until he was drafted out of law school to serve in Tacoma, Washington, during the Korean War. She graduated in 1953, after three years. She went home to Chicago until they were married in a white wedding a year later, with my other roommate and me as her bridesmaids.

Helen

Helen entered Stanford mid-year with a baby blue convertible. People she hardly knew asked her for rides. I tried not to ask. She and Rhoda are lifelong friends. I have visited them many times in Los Angeles and in St. Paul, Minnesota. When I do, it is like we have never been apart. Ruth and her parents were wonderful to me. I spent many happy hours at their San Francisco apartment. My friend Jackie was Phi Beta Kappa, as was Rhoda. I really admired them.

Mike

One day I was downstairs in my dorm ironing when a girl answered my buzzer. The call was from my freshman boyfriend, Mike, who used to walk me home from Spanish every day. He had asked me out earlier that day as usual, but I had told him I had to study. She asked if I minded if she went out with him. I was surprised, but I said, "I don't mind." She was sexually active. Mike and I were always in the back seat talking while this woman necked with Mike's roommate in the front seat. After she answered my phone, I never saw Mike again. All my friends asked me what happened to Mike. When I told them about the buzzer, they dropped her fast.

Dan

One day as I was walking to Roble Hall for lunch with my friends, a boy named Dan, who was a hasher at Roble, rode up on his bicycle. He asked me, "How's Mr. Jones?" I said, "Who is Mr. Jones?" He said, "He's the mayor of Weiser, Idaho." He went on like that with, "Mr. Smith, the superintendent of schools in Weiser," etc. I tried to find out how he knew, but he wouldn't tell. Much later I found out he had written to the Weiser Chamber of Commerce to get the information. It was fun and flattering, but I had no idea of dating him. He didn't even ask.

I had a date with a Stanford law school student from Piedmont. My Aunt Ruby insisted that a high school senior, the daughter of her friend, visit me on that same weekend. I was annoyed, since I didn't know the girl or what to do with her. I asked my date if he would mind bringing along a friend so we could double date. He invited a freshman boy (whom his parents had told him to look out for, just like my parents always did). It was Dan. It turns out his family and the girl's family had been friends for years, and they knew each other much too well. Such was life in the California Jewish community.

Dan invited me to celebrate Passover at his home in Piedmont. I didn't go, because I never wanted to leave Stanford. If I had, I would have been at the house next door to my future husband's home and not even known. Since I wanted to stay on campus, I went to Hillel that Passover. There I danced and spent the evening with the cutest, freckled-face, red-headed boy. Jim spoke with a New York Yiddish accent like I had never heard in Idaho. The next morning, he invited me to church. He was Catholic!

William

I was insecure with the Jewish boys, although they were wonderful to me. William treated me so well as a friend. He lived in a big Gothic house across the street from my roommate's home in Beverly Hills. His father was a big builder on Wilshire Boulevard. He and my roommate's brother even gave me a birthday party. My present was my favorite thing, a book. I spent one Rose Bowl evening at his Gothic style home with my date. Dianne Feinstein was there with a famous college football player.

I was very upset when years later I heard William was engaged to a beautiful girl who was the president of the AEPhi sorority at UCLA. He broke the engagement because her father was in the furniture business and not social enough for his family.

I was aware of societal differences, but they didn't bother me until I was later told by a friend that *class counts*. When I was a new bride, I went to lunch with an old, divorced Stanford friend who told me, "I'm much more social than you are, and besides that I own an Appel." It really crushed me, as I knew few people in Oakland, where I lived at the time, and nobody who collected Cobra School art.

My older Stanford friend got over that, and years later we met again at a party. My friends insisted she had changed and wanted to see me. She had a darling new husband and had traveled to the same strange countries I had. They said she was more down to earth. They told me, "She buys her clothes at Costco and donates wheelchairs to the South American poor." We became friends again and remained so until she died.

I always felt I was classless because I came from Idaho. Nobody my age cared about it there or any place I went. I figured I wanted to be upper-lower or lower-upper, as I learned about it in sociology class. Later, my husband delighted in teasing me that I was, "middle-age and middle-class."

Foreign Students

A tall, turbaned man from Pakistan must have been a prince. I met him at the Cosmopolitan Club, Stanford's international student center. Getting to know him, I found he was as naïve as he was handsome. He had been married when he was three years old. I cooked biryani with him at a foreign student banquet. I kept up on the news from Lahore and cooked his recipe many times.

Soft-spoken, premed Mungai was a member of the Kenyatta family, notorious politicians in Kenya. In a mellow British accent, he told me about the Mau Mau and Jomo Kenyatta, who placed skulls over the doorways of their enemies before they killed them. All my friends were friends of Mungai. I dated him, but I was embarrassed, as we were of different races and people were not as accepting as they are now. People stared at us as we danced. He told me all about his life and his relatives. I loved talking to him. Several of my friends visited him and his family in Kenya after college graduation. I was never so lucky, although I met his daughter at MeraLee's mayoral inauguration.

A quiet Japanese girl gave me stationery and other presents from home. Two German Fulbright students came through Idaho when I wasn't home. An Israeli man told me it was "my responsibility to take care of him because I was Jewish." (I knew nothing about Israel or Judaism at that time.) He gave me Israeli jewelry. He was too aggressive for me.

I dated a handsome student from Israel named Yosi. He was part-Arab and very temperamental. After college a friend gave my Aunt Rita an introduction to Yosie. She visited him in Israel. He was so good to her. Aunt Rita said she was "charmed by him and his lovely family." Foreign students were my window to the world and one of my favorite memories of Stanford.

I was on the pre-registration committee my junior year. We greeted the new freshman class. I had to go back to school one week early. There, I met my ideal man. He was from Fresno, and his aunt was the first woman ambassador to Europe, at a time when women were barely considered. He called her "Aunt Frances." He was tall, handsome, freckled-faced, blond, and not Jewish. He could have had his choice of fraternities, as he was intellectually deep and from a prominent family in Fresno, but he chose the eating clubs which were more inclusive. He drove an old beat-up car and was very unpretentious. He took me to the Pebble Beach Country Club and the beach, and we went out several times. He was a freshman, two years behind me. I was embarrassed when he took me to the freshman parties. I was a junior. I was so young at the time and didn't realize the pleasures I was losing by limiting my vistas.

Ed (Eloise's husband)

It took years for Stanford to stop having registration on Rosh Hashanah, an important Jewish holiday when religious Jews stayed home or went to temple. My girlfriends and I went to temple faithfully once a year on Yom Kippur in San Jose. I paid my dues to Hillel, but my friends and I seldom went.

I was a sophomore when I went to my first dance at Hillel. Ed cut in on me. He lived in Palo Alto. He didn't go to Stanford. He seemed a little strange and quite jerky. I ditched him immediately. He kept cutting in again and again. Unfortunately, he had gotten my name. He had relatives in Baker, Oregon. He went into Globe Furniture and looked me up. I was appalled. I had forgotten about him. He brought me some junk jewelry.

He found Eloise at the furniture store. He and Eloise were both mentally challenged. They wanted to get married, but it was problematic. Ed and Eloise were married at the Fairmont Hotel. Claire, Berta, and I were her bridesmaids. Ed worked for Uncle Julien in the Baker store during the times between his many nervous breakdowns. He was another person for the family to support.

Ed and Eloise have two children, Davy (mentally challenged) and Alan. Ed and Eloise moved to Denver to be with Alan. Alan is now divorced. According to his aunt, Berta, he is adjusting. He visits his mother, Eloise, who was eighty-eight in 2019. She is blind and can't walk. Ed is dead, and Eloise's sister, Berta, and her darling husband, Don, fly to Denver every three months to be with her. Davy, Eloise' son, lives and works at a home for handicapped in Marin. Once each month, Berta takes him on trips and to her home for the weekend. It took me years of therapy to get over my guilt about being raised with Eloise and Uncle Sam's bullying.

Bob

One of my closest boyfriends, Bob grew up in Palo Alto. He was a student at Cal. He was so good to me, but he was pressing me to commit. I wasn't ready. He wanted me to transfer to Cal. I wanted to have a journalism career, graduate from Stanford, and travel the world. My family interfered and pushed hard for me to "play the field."

I dated Bob during my sophomore and junior years. His parents lived upstairs in the apartment house where my grandmother lived in San Francisco. That was where we met. The boys included him as one of our crowd when he visited me at Stanford. He would spend the night in their room at the dorm. His fraternity pin was "on the shelf waiting for me to accept it."

Bob was studying law and living in the Pi Lam fraternity at UC Berkeley with his friends. I studied a lot too, and sometimes in the law library at Cal on Saturday nights. He would leave Cal at 4:00 a.m., take the ferry to San Francisco to get his folks' car, drive down to Stanford to take me out back in San Francisco or to a fraternity party at Cal. Then he would drive me back to Stanford by my 2:00 a.m. curfew. After that he would take his folks' car back to San Francisco and take the ferry back to Berkeley. He also came down to Stanford after finals to drive me back to San Francisco to the bus for my ride home to Weiser. After he consulted with MeraLee, he found I didn't have a watch. He bought me one for Christmas. My mother made me return it. I was very sad. I cried, but he understood.

Bob's family knew Ed's family from Palo Alto. I had never told Bob I had a step-cousin, Eloise. He heard from his family that Ed was going to marry Eloise and that she was my cousin by marriage. He tried to warn me about Ed. I got very upset. He asked me many times about my life and if he could go to Weiser. I felt very uneasy, and I tried to quit him. I really liked him. I was young. It was a terrible problem for me.

Bob flunked out of law school after the first year. After I hadn't heard from him, I had called his mother to ask about his finals. She said he was "driving down to Stanford to tell me now." I was on a date with Yosi. He came down to Stanford unannounced. MeraLee and Len spent the early evening with him. I was halfway down Palm Drive when I made Yosi drive me back to the dorm. I felt guilty about leaving campus after I knew. Yossi got angry with me. He had a temper. Bob had already left Stanford by the time I made Yosi take me back. I felt terrible. I couldn't commit to Bob. I wasn't ready. Bob had told me, "I fear three things: flunking out of law school, being drafted, and losing you." He did all three. It was a very hard time for both of us.

Hula Dancing

IN 1952, MY SOPHOMORE FINALS were over. Bob was my boyfriend. He suggested I enroll at Cal for the summer session and stay at the I House with him, so I could investigate social work for a career instead of pursuing journalism. It seemed a good idea. I enrolled. I had loved most of my Stanford classes, especially Russian literature, English, and poetry. Psychology and economics were difficult, and I didn't want to be a teacher. I thought I'd try studying social work for the summer to see if it was suitable for me.

After finals, I slept all day at my grandmother's apartment. My mother flew down to San Francisco and surprised me. She had met a Stanford woman on the plane bound for a summer program at the University of Hawaii. When we met Mama at the airport, she told me I should change my plans and go to Hawaii. She talked about it all the way into San Francisco, where we went straight to the travel agent. To my chagrin, I took the last place in the program.

"Mama, I'm staying at the I House! I'm already enrolled at Cal."

"You studied too hard."

"I have a boyfriend at Cal."

"He can wait!"

"I've packed my suitcase for Berkeley."

"You can unpack."

"I don't have a bathing suit."

"You can buy one."

"I don't want to go!"

"They have one space left in the program."

"All the good classes are full."

"You're going!"

I couldn't fight her. She was determined and controlling.

"Don't read a book. You read too much already."

"OK"

The I House was over!

That midnight, I left on a small propeller-driven plane. Bob was at the airport. The young pilot invited me into the cockpit at 5:00 a.m. to see the blue water and tiny brown and green islands from the open pilot's cabin as the small single-engine plane was about to land on Oahu.

We were greeted with orchid leis and housed in a motel two blocks from Waikiki beach. I was sad. I didn't know my two new roommates. I missed the I House and Cal. Only two classes were open to me at that late date, hula dancing and Stanford Professor Emeritus Graham Stuart's class on reading modern plays.

In the end I had a blissful summer in Hawaii. The day I arrived, my family ordered me to call a wholesale jeweler related to my mother's cousin, Marie. He insisted, "Come to dinner tonight." I was tired. I had been up since 5:00 a.m. He wouldn't let me say no. I took a taxi to his spectacular modern home on the hill. Over drinks, I noticed the floor-to-ceiling glass shelves in front of the windows overlooking the tropical forest and ocean were loaded with Japanese netsukes. His charming, redheaded wife wore a purple and green muumuu brightly patterned with large exotic birds and plants.

After cocktails he gathered his ten guests and took us by bus to a tropical garden for a luau complete with ukulele music and dancers. My host probably didn't entertain again until ten days later when another group of jewelers came to Oahu. I had nothing to do with jewelry. He later invited me out on his yacht to greet the Trans Pacific Yacht Race. I bought a red-flowered bathing suit.

A New York family at the party had a daughter my age. They probably were jewelry buyers. They invited me to dinner at the Royal Hawaiian Hotel. I later had dinner with this young girl and her family in their lovely apartment in New York. I don't even remember her name. I'm so sorry I didn't keep up with her. I was really shy.

The next day, two cute sailors dropped by our apartment to take my roommates to Hanauma Beach. I was alone, so they invited me to come too. Since one of the sailors wore a huge Star of David, I decided to go. I took a book to read on the warm, white hill while they frolicked below in Hanauma Bay. The next day the man with the star asked one of my roommates out. The cute, curly-haired Catholic sailor asked me.

It was a young and glorious summer. Sailor Ed had no money. He was an artist from a poor part of eastern Pennsylvania. Barefoot, we painted beside the warm water under the palms on Waikiki Beach. We danced freely every night beside the waves, beneath the huge Banyan tree at the old Moana Hotel. We saw floor shows at the Royal Hawaiian by craning over its outside walls from the sand under our bare feet. We knew we were "going to the Hukilau," as we watched the swaying dancers in grass skirts and leis moving their bodies and fingers to the tunes of flower-shirted Hawaiian men playing ukuleles.

Thin, brown-skinned local boys would shimmy up palm trees to get us coconuts and try to impress the girls during our outdoor hula classes. With bare feet, in my red-flowered bathing suit, I was not only uncoordinated, but very distracted. (I think I read later that one of them was Daniel Ken "Dan" Inouye, a United States Senator from Hawaii from 1963 to 2012. He was a member of the Democratic Party and president pro tempore of the United States Senate (third in the presidential line of succession from 2010 until his death in 2012). He was the highest-ranking Asian-American in the Senate.

The university supplied army-officer escorts for the young college girls. The blond, white, uniformed man who drove me around the island, showing me the other side and the Japanese Golden Pavilion, seemed really old and boring to me compared to sailor Ed.

I loved exploring Honolulu. I visited all the museums, including the Museum of Fine Arts and the interesting Hawaiian History Museum. Besides King Kamehameha, Hawaii for me was body surfing, shell collecting, dancing, painting, and an excursion to the Island of Kauai, where in our wet bathing suits we slid on enormous flat green tea leaves down the rain-soaked hills and waterfalls.

My grandmother, Mollie, came to Hawaii on the famous boat, the *Lurline*, a week before my classes ended. She stayed at the old Moana Hotel. That was the end of my summer romance with the sailor! I didn't see Ed again until he bid me "aloha" from a distance as the ship slowly sailed from shore.

There were three hundred young women and three men sailing home on the *Lurline* that day. One of the men was my charming seventy-five year old drama professor emeritus, Graham Stuart. I tried very hard to fix him up with my grandmother, but I think he was interested in me!

My boyfriend, Bob, met me at the dock. I have only palm-filled watercolors, a red bathing suit, and memories of my spectacular summer in Hawaii. Stanford has no transcript of my summer session at the university because *I flunked hula dancing!*

Kurt

IT WAS 1953. I WAS in my junior year at Stanford. The topic of the noon YWCA discussion group was the rebuilding of Germany. The German students were invited. I grabbed a sandwich and went. During the discussion, one of them said, "We've had a war, but now we must let bygones be bygones and start anew." I roused from my noontime fatigue and thoughtlessly said, "How can you forget a war? Think of the people who were killed." A gasp went through the room. All eyes were on my insult. The German students were our guests. I knew little about the Holocaust at the time. I quickly ran home to my dorm and cried in shame.

I studied alone in the stacks of the old main library. Suddenly, a young, wavy-haired, blond man was there and every place I went. Finally, he said, "I want to talk to you." His name was Kurt. He was from Bonn and had been thirteen years old at the time of the Fuhrer. His father was in the printing business. His family was against the Nazis. They listened to the Voice of America on short-wave radio and heard stories of Germans making "soap" out of Jews. They felt that "such statements were enemy propaganda designed to weaken the morale of the German people." They refused to believe what they heard.

Kurt was a rebellious youth and a member of the young Brownshirts, a broad Nazi movement of political indoctrination of German children. They marched to martial music and saw movies of Hitler kissing young children and looking at birds. He told me, "You can't blame the children."

The war was over, and he was at Stanford on two scholarships, one a Fulbright. He had earned his way through school by working night and day as a streetcar conductor in Bonn.

He seemed truly sorry about the Holocaust, very repentant and remorseful. He wanted to meet Jewish students to get to know them and atone for Germany. He seemed sincere. He was handsome, as blond Lutheran boys often are.

The memory of the war was still raw. Americans were not friendly. He found solace with the other German students. My circle of friends was largely Jewish. We believed him and tried to accept him as a friend and learning experience. Later, one of my girlfriends even stopped by Bonn to visit him. She stayed in his home after graduation on her way to a master's program at the University of Jerusalem. She later told me she was uncomfortable being in Germany with his family.

Kurt and I researched the propaganda section of the Hoover Library. There, we came across political cartoons of tiny, fat American airplanes coming down to bomb the innocent men, women, and children of Nazi Germany. The noses of the airplanes were caricatures of the face of Franklin D. Roosevelt. We found the identical drawings from an American newspaper, but the face was that of Adolph Hitler.

I was studying *Faust* in a small student seminar in a professor's home. I told Kurt about the class. The teacher read to us in German and English. Kurt and I sailed rowboats on Lake Lagunita and read Goethe together. I loved Goethe. I still can quote the poetry from *Faust*, it was so appealing to me:

> Oh, give me back that time of pleasure,
>
> When yet in glorious youth I sang.
>
> When like a font the crowded measure,
>
> Uninterrupted gushed and sprang.

> When bright mist veiled the world before me,
>
> In opening buds a marvel woke,
>
> Which every valley richly bore me,
>
> As I the thousand blossoms broke.

TRAVELS WITH AN ARTIST

I nothing had,

And yet enough for youth.

Joy in delusion,

Ardent search for truth.

Oh, give me back that old emotion,

The bliss that touched the verge of pain,

The strength of youth, love's deep devotion.

Oh, give me back my youth again.

J.W. von Goethe

Our friendship was platonic, soul-searching, and exciting. One evening Kurt came to my dorm carrying an armload of long, bare, black branches. Those pink cherry blossoms bloomed in my room all spring.

Kurt was planning to herd sheep in Nevada during the summer. The experience was not what he expected. The sheep herders were unexpectedly rough. They spoke in monosyllables, and very little at that. Dirty and bearded, they went into town on Saturday nights to drink their paychecks. They would scream, "Haaaa!" and prod their pointed rods at the sheep, which would slowly saunter and move. It wasn't at all like Beethoven's "Pastoral," or "The Passionate Shepherd," as he might have imagined.

He decided to hitchhike to Weiser. I didn't know he was coming. He slept one night in the jail in Winnemucca and arrived unannounced at my mother's door the next afternoon. She was not thrilled. We were one of five Jewish families in our small, unworldly Idaho town. She couldn't understand why "a young Jewish girl would go to college and bring home a German." She didn't relate at all to the handsome young man who came to call.

My stepfather was in the furniture business. My mother sometimes went to church socials to explain the Jewish holidays and set holiday tables. She had run a Sunday school in her basement for the five or six Jewish children in town. My mother felt like an outsider in the largely Episcopalian and Mormon community. She felt her Judaism very strongly.

Kurt read his paper to my family on his conviction that not all the German people were to blame for the Holocaust. My parents were not convinced. My stepfather invited him to speak at the Lions Club. The Lions, also, were unconvinced. The Metropole, the only soda fountain in town, had a sign outside its door that said in big letters, "NO JAPS." I felt my father and the town were prejudiced, intolerant, unreasonable, dark, and very unwelcoming. I felt my stepfather was the ultimate "Jew". Those were strange times.

After four days, I was told by my family that it was time for my guest to be leaving. I broke the news to him while we were picnicking on an island in the Snake River. Kurt left, but before he did, he said to me, "You've got to get out of Weiser, Helen Ann, or you're going to end up with a *house full of furniture*." That scared me so much I left.

While I was at Stanford early that fall on the pre-registration committee, two other German students drove through Weiser. I was not home, but my mother entertained them and really enjoyed them. She put them up for the night. She found them refined, interesting, and intelligent. She probably wasn't threatened that I would get involved with them. She hadn't liked my friend Kurt.

I've been to Germany many times. When I was in Bonn, I thought about Kurt, but I could never reach him. One night my husband and I were sitting in a restaurant in Berlin. The young man sitting next to us offered to help us with the menu in English. We visited, and I told him about Kurt. He said, "I'll find him."

Late the next night, before our morning departure, the man from the restaurant came to our hotel. He had located Kurt in Frankfort on a list the German government keeps of all their citizens and had contacted him. He said Kurt was waiting for my call. It was eleven o'clock. I called, and we talked. Kurt said he was in the Indian-fabric importing business. His wife was an artist. His son lived in Oakland on Lenox Street. We invited him to call us when he was in town, but he never did. Maybe he didn't miss his youth, the youth that Goethe dreamed about? Maybe his interest and sympathy for the Jewish people was just a young man's ruse? Maybe he didn't like me or Weiser hospitality? Maybe he was anti-Semitic after all??

Graduation

Graduation was great. MeraLee had been gone for a year, and my other roommate refused to go through the ceremony. I was left with my friends Helen, Rhoda, Ruth, Barbara, Jackie, and Dodie, and our parents. I talked my parents into staying in Palo Alto one more day after graduation so I could attend my friend Dodie's wedding at the Mark Hopkins Hotel. Then I found myself, tearful and reluctant, in the back seat of our car whirling back to Weiser. *I can't believe that happened!*

I wanted to be a journalist and travel the world like my beautiful cousin, Annabelle, who worked for the *Chronicle*. Economics and political science were hard for me at Stanford. I got a C in psychology. I ended up a history major. I should have majored in art history or English, which were better suited to my talents. That choice was not even presented to me. My mother wanted me to be a teacher, but the education courses were of little interest to me. I took them one summer to raise my grades.

In college, I dreamed of someday marrying a college professor, a politician, or a poet. I wanted to wear sensible shoes, read Proust, work for a newspaper, eat whatever I wanted (forgetting my weight), and discuss liberal politics and philosophy until late in the night.

My father had given me some money to go to Europe. I put down a deposit on a bicycle tour. My mother told me when I arrived back in Weiser, "Anabelle had a breakdown in

Europe, and Robert flew over to get her." That news stopped me. I spent the early part of the sad summer stuffing envelopes in the Globe Furniture Company. Uncle Sam said, "If you want to get married, your husband can work for me." I didn't have anyone in mind, and that would have been the kiss of death for any man if I had!

Claire

After two years at Finch College, Claire transferred to UCLA, where she majored in theatre and drama. She lost a part to Carol Burnett, who went on to fabulous fame. Claire had beauty and charisma. On a college break, Claire drove up to Stanford in her little turquoise convertible to see me. We filled it with boys and drove around the campus. We always had such fun together.

On a Bermuda break from Finch, Claire met a tall, handsome Jewish man by the name of Eugene Freedman. He was from Larchmont, New York, and he spoke with a heavy New York Jewish accent.

I had an invitation to be MeraLee's bridesmaid in September in Chicago. At the end of July, I stayed overnight with Claire's Aunt, Rose Marie Reid, in Los Angeles. The next day Claire, her younger brother, Sanny Jo, and I left for Washington, D.C., where Eugene was stationed in the navy during the Korean War. Claire was anxious to get to Washington in five days.

We drove old Route 66 in the little open car. A sudden arroyo shower delayed us over an hour in a golden rainbow of the Painted Desert. It was noon, and it was hot. Cars were lined up in both directions. After the long wait, we counted the cars in the opposite direction on the other side of the water. We gave the last car in line the sad number, one hundred, as we laughed and drove on.

I promised to meet a boyfriend, an author, at the post office in Tucumcari, New Mexico. He was in the army secret service. At the time there were no cell phones. After some negotiation with Claire, who was in a hurry to get to Washington to see Eugene, I gave him up so we could visit the Grand Canyon at dawn. I never heard from him again.

I remember the three of us singing while gliding by meandering lakes and the beautiful, green, forested Ozarks. The top was down, and our legs hung out. The little turquoise convertible sped along. Hillbilly music was on the radio, unlit corn cob pipes were in our mouths, and raggedy straw hats were on our heads.

We made it to Washington in five days. Sanny Jo left us in New York. Claire and I took an apartment for the month of August at Hunting Towers in Arlington, Virginia. She visited Eugene every day, and I walked around Washington by myself, visiting the marvelous museums and monuments.

One day I went to the FBI. I was appalled to see the huge black-and white blowup photos of Julius and Ethel Rosenberg at the entrance. They were put to death for their beliefs. How could this happen in my country? My friend Joan Marie Shelley's father, was a California senator at the time. He was a former mayor of San Francisco. She invited me to sit with her in the Senate balcony, where we watched Senator Joe McCarthy of Wisconsin filibuster Senator Wayne Morse of Oregon on the floor. It was the terrible time of the McCarthy "witch hunts." So many important people in the movie industry were named by their coworkers as communists or sympathizers. The communist threat was not unlike some of the terrible things that are happening today.

My mother gave me a beautiful ring when I graduated college. It was the ring she was given by her mother upon her graduation from college. It was silvery white platinum topped by two diamonds and a sapphire, or two sapphires and a diamond—I don't remember which. I loved it and wore it every day. In the Corcoran Gallery I put my hand under the restroom faucet. The ring was on my finger, but the top with the three beautiful stones was gone. Horrified, I retraced my steps, searching the streets, sewers, and all the places I visited. When I finally dragged myself back to our apartment that night, I called my mother. "Mama," I cried, "I lost the ring." "It's only material," she told me. I really felt her love, and I've never forgotten her statement.

Sometimes we double-dated with a sailor who was a friend of Eugene's. The problem was, Eugene refused to convert to Mormonism, and they broke up. Claire found herself going alone to Mutual meetings at the Washington Mormon Church. There she met Reed Benson, the son of the Secretary of Agriculture under Roosevelt. They dated for the rest of our stay.

On weekends we went to New York, at first to visit Eugene. One weekend I went to Boston to visit my Idaho friend, who was stationed nearby in the army. I stayed with a friend of my mother's in Newton, Massachusetts. My mother wanted me to marry my Idaho boyfriend and live in Idaho, but I really wanted a career. As she was helping me pack my clothes, she mentioned, "You could get married in this green dress." I told her I wasn't thinking of getting married at that time.

Claire and Eugene did not get married. I went to Chicago to be a bridesmaid in MeraLee's wedding, and Claire went home to Baker, Oregon. After a couple of months, Eugene flew west. He and Claire eloped.

They were married a second time in the Mormon Church in Salt Lake City. Claire's Jewish father, Sanford, was not allowed to attend, because he would not convert to Mormonism. Eugene converted. They now live in Utah, where he is a bishop and attends Mutual every week.

MeraLee's Wedding

MeraLee married Leonard in September 1954, after a year of separation. She worked in Chicago, while he was drafted into the army in Tacoma. They had an all-white wedding in the Sarah Siddons Room of the Ambassador East Hotel. My entire Stanford crowd was there. We went to her parties all over Chicago. Our Stanford roommate and I were the bridesmaids, wearing white, strapless, diaphanous gowns with matching stoles. MeraLee's best friend from Chicago was the maid of honor.

After the wedding I went to Milwaukee with two of my friends, Helen and Rhoda. My father, Joe, put us up along with my cousin, Barbara, in a hotel. My two friends went on to St. Paul, where my friend Rhoda later married Don Mains. My father promised he would take me to St. Paul while Helen was still there. Instead, I found myself in his car on the way to Peoria to meet the Silverstein cousins. After a couple of weeks, I flew to San Francisco, over my mother's objections. She wanted me back in Weiser.

Single in the City

It was nineteen fifty-four. What a time to be single in the city! Newspaper work was for me. I loved working on the Stanford Daily, the excitement, the deadlines, the people, the perks, the comradeship and the pure exuberance of being where everything was happening **and being among the first to know.**

I was interviewed by Caroline Drew, the society editor of the Chronicle when I arrived in San Francisco. "You must go to a small town, a provincial paper to get started." she said. *Which was more important, the job or the city?* I grew up in a small town!

San Francisco was the city of dreams. The beaches, the bay, the beauty was like no place I had ever been. I loved the Barbary Coast, the night clubs, the theater, the suburbs, the available classes and the museums. It was a giddy time for me. *You couldn't get a city big enough for me. It had to be New York or London or San Francisco!* College friends were in Los Angeles but I had no reason to be there. I had family and connections in the city.

The Residence Club on Powell Street on Nob Hill was a perfect place for young single ladies. I had never lived on my own. You had to wear nylons and skirts every day and sign in at a certain time in the evening.

I took my first job with J. Walter Thompson, the advertising agency for Mattel Toys, Shell Oil and many other really well-known clients. The hours were nine to five, but don't believe it. The office was in a large gray stone building on California Street in the financial District. The problem was, there was a "glass ceiling." This was the early 1950's and all the copywriters were pale, white men. My pay check was a mere two hundred twenty dollars a month. "Oh, well, I've got to start somewhere." I figured.

I walked to work, watching the view of the water and the beautiful Bay Bridge. I passed Chinatown, where I bought pork buns in a storefront shop and ate them ravenously as I ran down the hill every morning.

My boss, Shane, was a hard drinking, chain smoker who worked a regular twelve-hour day. She was unrelenting with the client's orders that she put on my desk for me to fill immediately. It was a sedentary job. Sometimes I even felt guilty about taking a lunch hour. I found myself rushing all the time. Busy streets, frantic people, deadlines, after hours, and fast lunches with friends. When we worked late on a deadline we were treated to Shroeders, an old faded German Restaurant, for a quick sauerbraten dinner before returning to work. I had barely time to get back to the Residence Club to sleep.

I did date. I knew people from San Francisco and from school. How frustrating it was to have my dates wait in the lobby on Friday nights to take me skiing or to have dinner with their folks. Even on a weekend when I was snowed in at Tahoe, I had to take the train back alone to San Francisco to appease my boss.

Still, it was San Francisco and I had the bay, the beach and my family. I stayed. I had dinner at my grandmother's several nights a week. That was expected of me. I took nighttime classes in advertising at Golden Gate University and a quiet young man picked me up after each class. He was so wrong for me that I finally said, "No more." I didn't see him for months until his mother came to town and, "wanted to see my grandmother." (They were not such good friends in Seattle.) It was a ruse. That started him picking me up from my class again.

I met a man. Stan was a tall, good looking chemist who was into the same books and lectures as I was at the time. I scrutinized him carefully. He was the man waiting in the lobby for me to meet his folks at his home for dinner on a Friday night. Unfortunately, I had to be late. Shell Oil changed its mind. It demanded my Friday night time until 9 p.m.

A cousin of Stan's and his wife were at the family dinner table. After dinner the four of us went to the Mark Hopkins for a drink. Stan waited too long for the cousin to pick up the check and I was embarrassed. That was not the kind of man I had wanted.

Stan was called into the army and stationed at Fort Ord. I went down there to see him with his parents and his beautiful sister. He wrote me a letter and proposed. He wrote, "You could give me everything I ever wanted."

* * *

I wanted to go to Europe. It was important to me to see what was beyond my scope. I had tried several times before, unsuccessfully, to go. but now I had a job. I was invited to join some friends for a three-month European tour by private car with student drivers. My mother said, "You must come home to Idaho for a few weeks first." I was an obedient daughter.

Stan came home to San Francisco to see me on his first furlough carrying roses. I said to him, "Guess what! I'm going to Europe." He sulked all evening and the next day. He could have said. "Go and have a great time and we'll talk later" The proposal was not mentioned again.

I quit my job after seven months. It was not a distinguished career. I knew I'd do better next time. I first went to Idaho to visit my mother and step-father as my mother demanded. I had a bank account from my father, Joe, to pay for the trip. I used it.

I met Stan in New York with my father. He came down from Massachusetts where he was stationed and we spent the day together. My father was hesitant about him, but he said nothing. As I sailed past the Statue of Liberty, I was heady with joy and freedom. I forgot all about Stan. We wrote a few times. He took his furlough in October, thinking I'd be home, but I went back to Idaho until December.

I met him again on my second time in San Francisco. He came by my office two years later. Many things had happened in-between. I had broken an engagement that was announced in the San Francisco papers. He must not have read about it.

We went to dinner, but I had changed. I didn't want to discuss great books and philosophy all night. I had the best opportunity to compare him to Norman. Norman was cute and very smart. He made me feel good and he was so much more fun. Norman said,

"You'll be happy." *I wanted to be happy.* I was lucky.

London, Alone

I WAS IN LONDON IN 1956, alone and twenty-two. My three friends boarded the boat for the five-day trip home to America without even enough money for drinks. I waved them off, but I was lucky. While we were in Denmark, my father surprised me. He telegraphed me two hundred dollars. That was enough extra money to enable me to spend three more weeks in London at the end of the tour and to buy two dresses and a necklace in New York when I returned.

About a month earlier, I was holding tight to the ceiling straps of a crowded local bus climbing high above the French Riviera when I met a woman. She gave me an idea. She was staying with a family in Nice through an organization called *En Famille*. She offered me the address.

I wrote to them and found a place to stay in London. I told my mother, "I missed the boat." She answered, "You get on the next one!" The only ship I could change to easily was scheduled to sail three weeks after my friends left.

We had already visited the changing of the guards, Buckingham Palace, the National Gallery, Fleet Street, St. Paul's Cathedral, Trafalgar Square, and other points of interest. I traveled light, with only one suitcase. I threw most of my worn, wash-and-wear clothes away, as London was cold. I bought a beautiful gray flannel suit at Fortnum and Mason and probably saw a play. I knew no one in London. A family friend, a classmate from Stanford, took me out the first night. He left for home the next day. *I was alone!*

Did I do the right thing? My self-doubt came on like a bomb! I was so far from home, without even friends or family.

What if I had an accident?

What if I broke my leg?

What would I do if I lost my money and my passport?

Who would I talk to? At least they spoke English in London.

I was alone in a strange country! A German girl and two Belgian girls who never spoke to anyone were rooming in the upstairs flat on Mount Street where I stayed. The landlords, a thin, high-strung mother and a nervous curly-haired daughter, were French. They told me, "All the large department stores in London are owned by Jews."

This flagrantly untrue, anti-Semitic statement made me cringe, especially because I knew Fortnum and Mason, Harrods, as well as many other London stores, were not. Still, I stayed, as I had nowhere else to go. The cheap rent included a breakfast of thin, dry white toast, jam, and tea.

Mount Street was near the edge of Hyde Park and a few blocks from Marble Arch, designed by John Nash in 1887 for royalty to pass through on their carriages on the way to Buckingham Palace. All kinds of orators and eccentrics vented their platforms there before hecklers and onlookers every Sunday.

I went alone to the museums and sights of London. I remember the Sadler's Wells ballet. I took the floozy French landlord's daughter to the National Theater, where we saw my first Berthold Brecht play, *Mother Courage*.

One day the lovely German girl and I took the train to Cambridge. She fixed me up with a young German man, and we double-dated for a dinner at the famous restaurant, Simpson's on the Strand. The upstairs room and dinner were plain. We feasted on overdone, fried fish and chips, but I could feel the coldness and antagonism of staring people sitting around us. The memory of the war was still fresh in 1956, and their feelings ran deep. I could not go out with the Germans again.

I was seven or eight years old during the war. I lived in America. I was far away from their trauma. The bombing of London, the Blitz, was in 1940 and 1941. I saw the uncleared rubble, piles of bricks, and the gray, desolate bombed-out buildings. Weeds were growing out of their rough, slanting, shoulder-high walls and sides. Most of the ruins hadn't yet been cleared. Enormous broken rocks were strewn all over. It is hard to grasp the enormity of the suffering of the British people during those years.

London was a treat. I saw my entire history of painting class in the National Gallery. It was such a pleasure to see paintings by Leonardo Da Vinci and Titian in person. I loved the vestiges of British Royalty, the jewels, and the knight's armor in the Tower of London. I was disturbed by the story of the little princes in their cells, as well as the guillotine that cut off Queen Anne Boleyn's beautiful head. I loved the Japanese pagoda in the Royal Botanic Gardens at Kew and the flowers in the gorgeous, glass greenhouse that reminded me of the smaller greenhouse in Golden Gate Park, San Francisco.

I rode double-decker buses and saw the glorious, gourmet underground food stalls at Harrods. I climbed to the top of the dome of Christopher Wren's St. Paul's Cathedral, and I even made it by bus to Kenwood House at the edge of Hampstead Heath. I wandered the parks, antique shops, and neighborhoods. I climbed Blueberry Hill. I saw the statue of Franklin Delano Roosevelt in Mayfair's Grosvenor Square, donated in appreciation for his help in the Battle of Britain. I loved central London and especially Mount Street and Hyde Park, where I stayed. Every corner held a new surprise.

Walking around the museums, especially the Wallace Collection, men loitered around me. They were very knowledgeable about the art, discussing the paintings with great insight. One of them handed me a phone number and said, "If a woman answers, hang up." One man, a young German, wanted to meet me at the ballet. I pondered if I could meet him there, sit with him, and leave him after it ended. I was so young, lonely, and naïve.

I mentioned to the German follower that I had seen an identical painting in the National Gallery in Washington, D.C. He told me, "I wouldn't be surprised if America would steal all of Europe's treasures." I made the mistake of giving him my phone number so I could make up my mind if it was safe to meet him for an afternoon only in the theater. My landlady answered the phone when he called and asked me where I had met him. She almost threw me out! London is a big city, and you have to be very careful. Of course, I didn't meet him.

J. Walter Thompson had an office in London. Before I left, I had given them my final notice, but they told me to call their office when I arrived. I couldn't work in London because I wasn't British, and you had to have special papers. They had a lady in the London office who was a greeter. She took me to afternoon tea.

Tea was the national pastime in London. It was served daily, punctually at four o'clock at one of the grand hotels near Piccadilly Circus. We wore suits, high heels, silk stockings, hats, and gloves. We indulged on jam and cream scones, deviled egg and cucumber sandwiches, "spotted dick" (a traditional fruit or savory pudding), and exotic teas with milk and sugar—anything to spoil our dinner or substitute for it. The rooms were always lovely, and they often had teatime music, such as a harp or piano. It was the ladylike thing to do at the time. Men enjoyed it too.

My glamorous cousin, Anabelle, worked as a reporter all over Europe. She sent me an introduction to a charming, young South African couple. They worked for Reuters, an international news organization. They invited me to breakfast at Fortnum and Mason, my favorite department store. They spoke with the most melodious South African accent. They offered to take me to an audience with the Queen twelve days hence. Unfortunately, my boat left in ten days. I had promised my mother I would be on it, and I was unable to accept. I've never seen the Queen.

My grandmother had a San Francisco acquaintance who was from London. I had once dated their son. He was too old for me. She had me look up her friend's family. I met them in the last two weeks of my stay. The Sklans were orthodox Jews. They were very concerned that I was a young Jewish woman living with a gentile family. They wanted me to move in with them in Wembley Park, a suburb of London. I thanked them, but I was already settled in the center of town.

I did take the tube out to Wembley for Sabbath dinners the last two Friday nights of my stay. They didn't drive on the Sabbath, and I had to venture to the suburbs alone. They told me stories of living through the Blitz. The family lived in the center of London during that time. The sirens would blast every night, and everyone would run to the closest underground tube, grabbing their coats, blankets and pillows. They would have to descend long flights of stairs. There, they would try to sleep on the floor, underground, with the smells, dogs and cats and different people all crowded together. Some of the people were sick. There were no underground restrooms. The all-clear blast would sound every day around dawn. After they climbed the stairs, they would emerge drowsily from the station to see what buildings were still standing, what bodies were in the wreckage, and what was left of their homes.

Eventually the Sklan family moved to the north of England for the rest of the war. They knitted sweaters and caps for the soldiers to wear. Their brother was in the RAF, flying bombing missions over Germany. They didn't know where he was. They didn't hear from him for the entire length of the war. They worried and wondered if he were alive or dead. There was so much red tape they weren't able to find out. There were no lights after dark, as there was a curfew. Provisions were rationed, and they didn't have enough food on the table. Fortunately, they survived.

The Sklan family was so good to me. The aunt came into London two or three times to take me to lunch. I couldn't even do all of my planned sightseeing. I was afraid I missed so much, but I was wrong. Their loving friendship was one of the most precious experiences I took out of London. Eventually, I lost touch. I corresponded with them for a long time. Many years later when I came to London with my husband, Norman, I was able to take them out for dinner, at a kosher restaurant, of course.

Alas, my three extra weeks in London came to an end. As I sadly sailed from Southampton, I thought of the people, the paintings, and the history. I felt I had an education that I could never have had in school. I vowed I would go back to London the very next year. It took me over seventeen years to return.

When I came home from Europe, I moved to an old apartment on Union Street with a friend from Stanford. She had a car, and she taught me to drive. I took a job with Thomas Cook Travel agency. It was a good job for me. I had just come home. I was off at 5 p.m. I had enough time to enjoy San Francisco.

I had an usher's pass at the opera house. The first night after I found out, I ushered in a red plaid suit. I saw all the operas that season after my work. I was assigned to the topmost balcony. Almost everyone there was a musician except no-talent me. They either played an instrument or sang. I shyly asked a cute young man what he played. He answered, "I listen very well."

How I met my Husband

I WENT TO A PARTY IN Piedmont. I wore a bright yellow dress. It was different from what I would have worn in San Francisco, bouffant, sleeveless, and with a cinched-in waist. I bought it on my lunch hour from a store named Joseph Magnin, something I had never done before. *Why did I buy it?* I had no place to wear it.

It was a Saturday night in May or June of 1956. I was twenty-three. I had come back to San Francisco from my vacation in Weiser one day early for a party. My escort was a man named Dick. The party was for his former fraternity brother from Cal. Neither of us had ever been to Piedmont. We knew nobody. Nobody spoke to us. The home was designed by William Wesley Peters, a former partner of Frank Lloyd Wright,

We were eating alone when a cute, curly haired man and his date sat down next to us. This was his home. I was told the family was in jewelry. I asked him if he knew my friend, Kathy, whose father was a jeweler in Oakland. He did. Afterwards, we met his parents. To make conversation I asked if they knew my Aunt Rita, who lived in Oakland at the time. They said, "Yes." The Jewish community was small.

On Monday morning, Aunt Rita called me at work. She said, "Norman Licht is going to call you. I want you to promise me you will go out with him." Aunt Rita was a *Yenta*. Every time she heard of a young single man, she thought of her two nieces, Berta and me. I reluctantly promised I'd meet him. I already had a boyfriend.

Norman called. We talked for more than half an hour. Classical music, books, lectures, poetry, politics, and travel were discussed. He told me about the books he had read. Norman had never been to an opera. Except for values, I didn't think we had much in common. Because of my promise to Aunt Rita, I agreed to have coffee with him ten days in the future. That night I became engaged!

Dick gave me a big diamond. He didn't buy it. He took it out of the family safe. Everybody wanted to see my ring. I was working for Thomas Cook at the time. My boss and my friends made a huge fuss over it. I thought I would be happy. There were showers and parties, a honeymoon plan, and a very foreboding mother-in-law-to-be.

I broke all my future dates. A man called and invited me to dinner and a show with his visiting parents. I said, "I know a woman. She's pretty and tall like you and has an outgoing personality." I knew this woman only through double-dating. I remember seeing her at the law library at Cal when I was dating Bob. I felt she was aggressive. They eloped in six weeks.

An important boyfriend of mine from Idaho and Stanford called from Winnemucca. We had dated through college and after. He was driving down to see me. *Was he planning to propose?* (I'll never know.) I said, "Guess what, I'm engaged!" I never heard from him again. I didn't appreciate the charming, conservative men I knew in San Francisco. I called Norman and broke our coffee date. Norman didn't know me. It didn't matter.

My friend, Ruth, gave me a shower. I received tea towels, can openers, measuring spoons, and spatulas. It was a giddy time I hardly remember. My fiance's mother insisted the announcement in the *Chronicle* say, "He was a fourth generation San Franciscan." My parents gave us an engagement party in Weiser. Dick's mother didn't like Weiser. We kept her playing bridge until she left two days early, after the party.

We had planned to take Dick to Payette Lake with my mother and stepfather, aunt, and grandmother. Uncle Sam suddenly refused to go. We went without him. Afterward, Dick and I left for San Francisco together. The engagement didn't work out, and I gave him back the ring.

We were planning to attend separate weddings on Labor Day weekend. Dick was to be an usher in Los Angeles, and my friend Lorna's wedding was down the peninsula. I had a date for Lorna's wedding before our engagement. Dick had asked me to go with him but bring along someone else (how old fashioned).

The woman I had introduced to her future husband asked if she could come along with us. At the last minute, she brought him also. She told me, "He invited himself." My friend Lorna's mother met me at the door, asking to see my big diamond ring. I was wearing gloves. I didn't want to tell Lorna on her wedding day.

On the way home, the woman suggested we stop by her father's medical office. She said it was "on the way." Her entire family was there. She proceeded to flirt with her new boyfriend, while my escort and I sulked in our seats. She even invited herself out on his boat! I would never have done that. I was a lady, and that was too forward for me. I was very uncomfortable. I had just broken my engagement. We were sitting there ignored. They eloped six weeks later.

I spent the next day, a long Sunday, alone, going to a movie, and listening to the opera records my wedding escort had lent me. I had quit all of my boyfriends. Nobody knew.

Norman

My mother came to town on Monday and told Aunt Rita. She immediately called Norman. The following Saturday night, I was out with Norman. We went to dinner with his friends, and he kept me talking until after midnight. I still decided I couldn't go out with him anymore, but he called me for the next Friday with tickets to a play I really wanted to see. I was available. I only had my usher's pass for Saturday nights.

A few weeks later, my boyfriend, Stan, got out of the army. He came by Thomas Cooks Travel Agency, where I worked. He must not have seen the engagement announcement in the *Chronicle*. I had a wonderful opportunity to go to dinner with him on Friday night and out with Norman on Saturday. I told my Aunt Ruby, "I have changed." I was no longer interested in discussing Plato and great books. I enjoyed the fact that Norman was so much fun, athletic, handsome, and caring about my comfort.

I tried to leave my job at Cook's when I first broke my engagement. My father suggested I accompany him to a cousin's wedding in the east. The manager talked me out of quitting. I stayed three more months and finally quit just before Christmas. Cook's was the right job for me after I came home from Europe. I was visible. It wasn't taxing, and I could relive Europe. I could usher at the opera house, and people could come by for lunch and coffee breaks. Norman came by often. A Stanford woman took my place.

I took a temporary job as a wrapper at Gumps. After Christmas I had a job offer at Young and Rubicon Advertising Agency starting in two weeks. Norman suggested we fly to Weiser while I waited. "We can visit your folks and take your family's car to Sun Valley to ski. The California snow isn't good." We had a wonderful time (separate rooms, of course).

Norman had a spontaneous sense of humor and wonderful repartee. Most of all, I noticed that he was joyful and really comfortable with himself and his large family. I thought, *There must be something wrong with him.* He had no hang ups! We talked until late at night in the snow-covered car. He said to me, "You'll be happy."

What's happiness? Who's happy? When we returned the car to Weiser, my mother begged me not to fly to San Francisco with Norman, but I did. "Promise me you will not get married," was how she said goodbye.

On the Friday before I was to start my new job, the job was cancelled. Norman sent me flowers. I easily found a job at another ad agency: Batten, Barton, Burton and Osborne. Norman asked me to go with him to a jewelry show in Los Angeles for three days over Washington's Birthday in February. I would be staying with his sister, Gloria, in Ontario. It was all on the up and up. I didn't know Gloria. I made the mistake of telling my mother.

"You're not flying all over the country with a man."

"Oh, yes I am, Mama!"

Before 6:00 a.m. the next morning there was a knock at my door. It was Mama.

"What will people say if they hear I came to town and you left?"

Who were these people? I can't believe that stopped me!

The Wedding

Norman went to the show in Los Angeles for one day. We got married three weeks later. He told me he had an important diamond event in April and had to be at work by then. I tried to quit my job. The company wanted two weeks' notice. They changed my job. It was exciting. I loved it. It was a difficult time for me. I was meeting new people. I was confused, accused by my mother of being on the rebound, pressured to marry Norman, and worried whether I was doing the right thing. I was enjoying such a wonderful time in San Francisco. Still, I quit the agency, because we wanted a honeymoon, and I was too new at the job to take a vacation.

The wedding was hastily put together at the Fairmont Hotel by my mother. Fifty of my family's friends and relatives and fifty of Norman's family were invited. I was allowed two friends, Jackie and Ruth. I found my wonderful, white wedding dress three days before the wedding. It fit.

My father wasn't invited. I was told by Uncle Sam, my stepfather, he wouldn't give me a wedding if he came. My mother didn't have room for my roommate, MeraLee, in whose wedding I was a bridesmaid. She came up from Los Angeles with her husband, Len, the week before. I introduced them to Norman. I invited them anyway. She said she couldn't come at such a late date. Norman seemed very young and unsophisticated next to them. It took a long time before we resumed the close friendship we have had for years.

I struggled with my values and those of my family: prestige, social climbing, meeting important people, education, and culture. It wasn't the money. I didn't think about money at the time. I wanted to marry a college professor or someone who would change the world. I wanted be a reporter, to travel and write about it from distant places. I'll never know what I might have missed, not being in academia, knowing presidents and politicians, or visiting the White House.

I was told by my mother who my bridesmaids would be. My cousin, Joan Adler, was pregnant, and we weren't friends at the time. My other cousin, Berta, from the University of Washington, I hardly knew. They both refused. Norman's sister, Beverly Bloch, was my matron of honor.

My mother was still worrying about my marriage in the bridal room at the Fairmont Hotel when there was a knock on the door. Norman had sent me an exquisite string of pearls. I wore it when I walked down the aisle. My mother was happy for me. I felt sad that it had never happened that way for her.

It was a wonderful wedding. I first saw my stunning diamond wedding band when Norman kissed me and held me close under the Chuppah. We slept that night on the fifteenth floor of the Sir Frances Drake Hotel, high above the radiant, rainy, illuminated city. Norman remembered my twenty-fourth birthday the next day, March fourth, with a pink cashmere sweater in the bottom drawer of the dresser.

Norman and Helen Ann   March 3,   1957

We left the next day for our honeymoon in Mexico City. We visited my Aunt Belle's friend, William Spratling, who started the silver works in Taxco, at his home with his impressive Pre-Columbian art collection. We drank frozen daiquiris in Vista Hermosa, completely forgetting about the water. Norman paid a young man to get me up on water skis for my first time in Acapulco. I knew from the wedding night onward it was right.

Norman's family gave us a beautiful reception with all of my friends when we arrived home. We are now celebrating our sixty-third anniversary.

International Hospitality

NORMAN AND I WERE IN our thirties in the 1960s. We lived in Montclair in a small gray house in the Oakland hills with our two rambunctious little boys, David and Bruce. Our furnishings were sparse—a couch, a table, a TV, and very little else. Our home was lovely.

When I offered to drive my mother around Piedmont to look at all the beautiful homes, like she used to do with me when I was young, she didn't want to see them. I felt sorry for her. My Stanford friend, Jackie, told me, "Of all my friends from college, you have the nicest home and the nicest husband." Because of my mother's constant worry and running me down about getting married, those words meant a lot to me. Norman worked hard in the family jewelry business.

We loved to entertain. Some of our favorite guests were from the International Hospitality Center, an organization that welcomed foreign visitors to the Bay Area by matching them up with locals for home dinner visits. It was a continuation of my college interest in foreign students. Many of our friends were interested also, and we often entertained with other couples. Norman enjoyed those visits as much as I did.

We cooked for a beautiful Brazilian dancer, who really wanted to help with the dishes, although she seemed to have had many servants herself. My two little boys acted up when they were put to bed and cried and cried. They jumped up and down in their beds, so she saw the chaos of a real American household.

Another time we entertained a sophisticated, fashionably dressed French student, who said his family raised escargots beneath their home. He was so worldly that he wasn't interested in us or the children at all. We never heard from him again.

One time two soft-spoken Nigerian men with bulbous, ritual-scarred faces came to visit. One of them was the Secretary of Agriculture. They were dressed in the colorful flowered batik robes and red-and green-patterned woven hats they wore in their capitol, Lagos. They told us they had worn their national outfits instead of American clothing in America ever since they were refused a seat at a cheap breakfast counter in the South because they were black. We were so sad to hear about it.

Unfortunately, our water heater overflowed the day they were supposed to come. One of our friends was delighted when we had to ask her to move the dinner to her home. We all laughed together and had a wonderful time despite hearing about their disturbing American experience.

We had our difficulties. One evening when we were entertaining with another couple, our guest was to be a charming Englishman, Benedict Nicolson. He was the publisher of the *Burlington Magazine*, a prestigious literary and art magazine in London. We and our friends knew little about him. I had seen his beautiful, classical art magazine in a bookstore once. I later learned, via Wikipedia, he was the son of the late Sir Harold Nicolson and the Bloomsbury writer, Vita Sackville-West, the consort of Virginia Woolf; and the brother of Nigel Nicolson, a British Conservative Member of Parliament.

He was a tall, elegant gentleman with a quiet, cultivated English accent. I found out later that he had grown up in Sissinghurst Castle outside of London, where the beautiful gardens were later opened to the public by the National Trust. I saw his castle later in a movie on Virginia Woolf.

It must have been a real come-down to be in our little house. He didn't brag about himself. He said our small home was "so lovely." He asked all about us and our family in a refined, beautiful British accent.

We knew the *Burlington Magazine* he edited and published was very important, and *so was he*! It was an experience I'll never forget. We later found out his portrait, photographed by Lord Snowden, now hangs in the National Portrait Gallery in London.

At the last minute the Hospitality Center called us with a desperate plea. "We have a doctor from Pakistan who has nowhere to go. Please, please, please, have him over with your English guest." We should have said no. We didn't want to have him. *What could we do?* They insisted he had no other place to go. We said, "Sure."

It was 1963, and President Lyndon Johnson was entertaining an indigent, unlettered Pakistani camel driver at the LBJ Ranch that same week. The story was printed in big headlines on the front page and all over the *Chronicle*.

The short, swarthy doctor came to our home. He was very dour and upset when he saw our "little home". "The ignorant camel driver was being royally entertained by the President of the United States!" He talked about it all evening. He probably felt it should have been him. We served hors d'oeuvres, wine, and a lovely dinner. The table was decorated with candles and multi-colored flowers.

On one of his toasts, the doctor lifted his glass and loudly exclaimed, "Hey, Englishman!" without mentioning Mr. Nicolson by name. He didn't know the magazine and wasn't interested in him at all. Our refined English guest seemed graciously not to hear.

By the middle of the repast, the four of us were so embarrassed by the Pakistani doctor's constant rudeness that we decided we couldn't send the two men home together in one taxi as we had planned. They didn't mix! Our friends had the task of driving them both back to their San Francisco hotels. My husband and I ended up doing the dirty dishes alone.

Before our daughter, Lisa, was born, we moved to Lafayette. It was too far from San Francisco for the guests to commute, and the BART transit system was not developed at the time. We thought it would be a wonderful experience for our children to meet visitors from other countries.

We joined the faculty wives at the University of California. Through them, we entertained a young, Chinese Cal student from the Philippines named Benito. He came to our home often during his four years at Berkeley. "My father is in business, as are most of the Chinese people in the Philippines," he explained. He really missed his family, and he fit well into ours. He went with us to my art shows and on many excursions. One day he visited our son's school to talk to the children about the Philippines, bringing a bamboo flute, some batik material, a small wooden ox, and some coins.

An arrogant French girl lived with us for a week. She asked my daughter to iron her clothes. My teenage daughter did not like her and did not want to have anything to do with her. It was probably a difference in cultures. My daughter was very unhappy during this visit, and it was really hard. The French girl invited us to visit her in Paris, but we never did.

Two young Japanese boys of our sons' age spent three weeks with us one summer. We learned origami, and they learned to play baseball. On the last Sunday, we were taking our son and his friend to their summer camp at Stanford. We wanted to take the boys too, but we had already promised to take my son's friend and all their luggage. There was no room in our car. Our Japanese gardener met them and invited them to a baseball game and dinner that day. That really helped us. They had such a good time.

The Jewish Welfare Federation called us about an Israeli family who were lonely because they didn't know anyone. Rafi, the father, was studying for his PhD. in Chinese art history at Cal, and the family of four was living in student housing in El Cerrito. We became good friends. I visited their daughter when she was in the hospital for a short time. They were here for three years, with one year away in Formosa.

They came for Thanksgiving dinner when they returned from Formosa. They were carrying a large, indigenous painting of a Formosan aboriginal wedding. It occupies a special spot in our living room. Rafi taught on the *Semester at Sea*, the boat that took high school students around the world for credit. He wasn't allowed to debark in Indonesia because of his Israeli passport.

They asked us to dinner at their student apartment. By then they knew many local people. There we met one of the leaders of the San Francisco Jewish community. After his Ph.D., Rafi was invited back to San Francisco often to speak about Israel for the Jewish Welfare Federation. We saw him whenever he was in town.

We visited them in their home in Israel, where Rafi was a professor at the University of Jerusalem. Two of our children went to Israel on temple programs. Rafi and his family met them and entertained them in their home. We love visiting the people we have met in their homes abroad. We are grateful we have had so many opportunities.

Painting

I WAS AN ORGANIZATION WOMAN, PRESIDENT of Hadassah, president of Ort, and very involved in Democratic Party politics. By 1961, we lived in Lafayette. I had one day free with help, Tuesday. For three years I left my children and spent that morning at the first docent class at the Oakland Museum. We learned about twentieth-century art and the California missions. After the morning class, I ate a sandwich in the car on my way to Lundy Siegriest's afternoon painting class.

I took the class with some friends at Civic Arts in Walnut Creek. My friend Beverley and I continued in Lundy's class for years. He hardly taught. Lundy regaled the adoring ladies with stories of his drinking and carousing. Once in a while he would say, "Put some blue in that corner," or "Stop right there." The talented ladies all loved him.

My first group show was outside Civic Arts. Two well-dressed men were vigorously discussing my large red-centered, ultramarine flower in its faux Renaissance frame. I dragged my father-in-law over to hear them, "Have you ever seen anything so terrible in all your life?" Red-faced, I let my father-in-law go back to the family.

I couldn't draw. I knew I was a fraud. I wanted to learn the basics. I wanted to go to a recognized art school. UC Berkeley was what I needed. Lundy said, "Don't go to school." It was 1974. I was showing my work at the Lucien Labaudt Gallery in San Francisco, where Richard Diebenkorn had his first show. Mrs. Labaudt also said, "Don't go to school." My children were in junior high and high school. I wrote a glowing recommendation for myself and handed it to Lundy. He reluctantly signed it. I was accepted into Cal on my paintings. At forty years old, I received two second degrees, one in studio art and one in art history.

I loved Cal. In my first year I took an elective sculpture class. I was friendly with a young man in the class. We talked all the time as we sculpted. He hurt his hand, and I rushed over to see if I could help. He turned on me with great vehemence. "Stop acting like my mother." That put me in my place.

I loved the sculpture class, but painting took over. I never felt I really fit in with the younger students. They had their parties, but I always had parties in Contra Costa at the same time. Professor O'Hanlon, my Cal sculpture teacher, as famous as he was, attended my show at the Labaudt Gallery.

I painted at Cal with some of the most important artists of the Bay Area Figurative school: Joan Brown, Elmer Bischoff, Karl Kasten, Boyd Allen, and many others. George Lloyd, my drawing professor, taught us to dip a tree branch in ink and sketch a figure. He didn't get tenure. When he left Cal, he joined my drawing group in Lafayette for a short time. Professor Karl Kasten became a family friend until he died. He never missed my shows. His home was full of wonderful ancient art and his own beautiful paintings. Norman and I just loved him. I still see my Romanesque art T.A., Dr Mary-Ann Milford Lutzker.

Italy

I had to take two art history classes along with painting classes to get my B.A. in studio art from Cal. One of the classes was Renaissance Art. As I was walking out of the lecture, I saw a poster for a summer school in Venice. I watched it for a long time: it could offer my second art history class.

In 1974 my husband was busy opening a store in San Jose. Of my three children, David was grown and away, Bruce was to be in Israel for the summer, and Lisa was to be in camp. Norman said, "Go". I went. I had not been to Europe since I was in London before I was married.

TRAVELS WITH AN ARTIST

I spent three days in Zurich, where the plane landed. Then I took the train to Venice. Mantua wasn't included—though it was close. I wanted to go there, but there were no train connections. I asked about it at the introductory class meeting. I wanted to see the Ducal Palace and attend the opera in the Arena in Verona.

A lady from Canada wanted to go too. She knew a driver from the Gritti Palace Hotel, where she had stayed. She seemed quite haughty as she looked me over. I wore only traveling clothes and no jewelry. She wore diamond rings and lots of jewelry. She told me her driver could pick us up after our group excursion to Verona. We missed the visit to the Venetian Arsenal the next day, but I made up for it later.

The driver met us at the end of the class in Verona and drove us to a hotel. While we were having a cocktail, I called the famous old Verona restaurant, The Twelve Apostles, and made a reservation.

The driver dropped us off in the deserted, cobbled, stone street in front of the restaurant and disappeared. Outdoor stands adjoined the entrance, full of colorful vegetables and fruits. Inside we saw a painted church-like ceiling. It was gorgeous. We could almost taste the aroma of olive oil, roasted meat, and garlic.

We walked in with much anticipation. The host greeted us and told us, "We have no room!" We had to leave. He said he told us when we called there was no room but we didn't understand. The driver was gone. We had no telephone. The street outside was empty, a desolate, lonely place on an unknown hill. We hobbled tentatively down an unknown pebbled street in our high heels.

While we were eating a sandwich in a drab downtown drug store and nursing our sore feet, we bonded. After seeing a glorious *Carmen* at the Roman Arena de Verona, our driver was waiting. We had to miss the vibrant nightlife of Verona and drive to Mantua in the dark. We saw the Ducal Palace and the Palace of the Giants the next day.

* * *

The seventeenth-century art class took us all over Venice. When I told the lovely woman living in the room next to me that Norman wrote, "The dog cries every morning when I put him out," she replied, "Better it than you!"

I met the wife of the retired gondolier. She leaned over her balcony all day watching as I sketched the church, the ancient well, and the School of the Shoemakers on our small square, Campo San Toma. She invited us upstairs into her dining room, where we sat around a lace-covered table beneath a twining, flower-filled glass chandelier as the painted Madonna smiled sweetly in her pink and blue robes from her spot above the half-burnt candle on the buffet. This was during the final project of our class in Venice. One of my friends dated the fourteen-and fifteenth-century buildings, and a third translated. We were preparing for our walk around Venice learning about the other small squares explored by other people on the last day of our class. I had wanted to take the Ghetto walk, but when the two ladies asked me to join them, I fell in love with Campo San Toma.

* * *

Two years later, I repeated my entire trip with my family. When I was in Verona with Norman, Bruce, and Lisa, we went back to The Twelve Apostles. The food was not good. It was faded, uninteresting, and way too expensive.

Helen Ann Licht Campo San Toma. 1974

When I returned to Cal, my husband and I were invited to our dashing middle-aged professor's home, where we met his twenty-three-year-old girlfriend. **Norman knew her mother!** She had met him at Harry's Bar in Venice, along with various counts, princes, and other important international people. I was happy for her, as I had also been in Venice at the time and I had met the wife of the retired gondolier.

UC Berkeley

THAT'S FOR ME, I SAID to myself as I passed the open door of Joanna William's Indian-miniature class and saw the radiant slides on her screen. The bright reds, blues, and greens reminded me of my own polychromatic paintings. I decided to go for a third B.A. in art history. That led to classes in Oriental art and travel to the Orient and India with my husband. After my third graduation, I took docent classes at the Asian Art Museum in Golden Gate Park. I was showing my work at Temple Emanu-el in San Francisco at the time. I was busy.

My parents died while I was at Cal. I sat in the hospital in Boise on weekends. I was all alone, with my art history books and notes. Joan Brown took me on independent study. My friend Dr. Mary Ann Milford was the teacher's assistant in my Romanesque Art class. She saved all the notes for me. My Japanese art professor was called to Japan for a week during that time and canceled a full week's classes. I felt it was meant to be. I canceled my offer to drive David Simpson to see my "Works on Paper" show at the Valley Art Center in Walnut Creek. When I came home after the funeral, Rabbi Shelley Waldenberg called me. I was lying on the bed.

"What time is your class?"

"Eleven a.m., but I'm not going."

"I'll come over at one."

I went to class that day. Mary Ann saved me the notes of the Romanesque class. I didn't learn anything. I felt like a ghoul. I got a C in my senior seminar, Peter Selz's outstanding class on Art Nouveau. I was advised by friends to tell him the awful news. I was embarrassed to do it. I went through the ceremony with my kids and a friend watching. He let me rewrite my paper after I had my degree, and he changed my grade. I was through with school. I went back to Lundy and painted with him until he died. He left me a beautiful painting of cows, his specialty.

I had a studio in Oakland. Whenever I stopped by my husband's jewelry store after a day of painting, Norman would grab my hand and say in front of the customer, "Show her your rings." My hands held the residue of paint below my paint-darkened nails. I put my rings back on whenever I left the studio.

Many shows followed: three at Stanford, three at Temple Emanu-el in San Francisco, little galleries, and Jewish centers. Three of my paintings hang in a tennis club in Tepotzlan, Mexico, following a show in Mexico City. I had three shows in the Marin Civic Center, I showed three times in the B'nai B'rith Klutznik Jewish Museum in Washington, D.C, and at Creighton University Art Gallery in Omaha, Nebraska. I had a beautiful show at the Bade Museum in Berkeley.

I showed twice at the Crocker Museum in Sacramento in the Kingsley-Crocker show. Joan Brown was the juror. Diablo Valley Hadassah led an art tour to Sacramento just to see my paintings. I recently showed at the Orinda and Lafayette libraries and I had a big one-person show at the Museum of Jewish Heritage in Danville.

One of my paintings, *Jacob and the Angel*, is in the virtual Midrash in Israel. I was scheduled for a fourth show at the Orinda bookstore in April as well as a temple tour of the art in our home. Both were canceled because of the coronavirus.

One of my favorite shows was in the Jewish Center in Walnut Creek. They gave me a beautiful reception, and the paintings showed so well. The whole room was filled with so many people I knew and loved. People even came from San Francisco. They stopped the show in the middle to present me with a meaningful metal menorah, and I sold the prize painting, *The Dance of Our History*, that was shown in the museum in Sacramento—that was the painting that Hadassah went to Sacramento to see.

My favorite shows were in my community with my friends. My old friends from Stanford came to my shows in Palo Alto. As a painter, I was invited to sit on the class panel for my fiftieth reunion. The other woman on the panel, Barbara Packer, raised six children, had her Ph.D., hiked the Himalayas, and was working an important job at Hewlett Packard. The four men on the panel were all important student and civic leaders, but nobody imagined that anyone could paint! Eight of my best friends and Norman sat in the second row. It was one of the highlights of my life.

Don Loze, who was on the panel, was the student body president at Stanford. He arranged a show for me in Temple Sinai in Los Angeles. Some of my friends came down to Los Angeles for the show. My friends from the south all came. My cousin, Charles Dolginer, bought an important painting, *Red Sea Crossing*. I asked him if he wanted a family discount, and he said, "No!" I still love seeing and trading paintings with many of the talented, supportive artists I know. I feel painting has been such an exciting and rewarding career.

In the airport, leaving Oaxaca, I sketched a remembrance of the Zocalo, the charming square in the center of town. I made a painting from the sketch, *On the Zocalo, Oaxaca*. It showed at Stanford. My gallery, Interart, placed it in the State Department's "Art in Embassies." It led to an important invitation to dinner at the White House during George Bush Sr.'s administration. Unfortunately, I didn't go. I protested the Viet Nam War. I made a big mistake. I'm sure it would have helped my career.

My son-in-law, Scott Danish, helped me make a book of my paintings, *The Many Colored Bible*. It is still on sale at Amazon.

My Blue Painting

The curatorial committee came to my home to pick out the paintings for my show at the Jewish Heritage Museum in 2018. I noticed on the Friday before they were to collect them that one of my earliest, pivotal paintings had to be framed. The people from the museum were going to pick up the show paintings a week from Monday. I never thought I'd show this painting, as it was so old. I looked at it again, and it was blue and beautiful. The temporary tape on the edges was coming off. *How could I get it done in such a short time?* I called what was left of my artist friends—they were older. They suggested only commercial places. My painting was an odd size, and it would take three weeks to frame. Also, the cost would be astronomical.

I finally found a framer who would frame it by the next Thursday if I bought cut wood at Ace Hardware. I did it! "Too bright," said the framer when I brought him the unpainted wood. "You must paint it first." I took the painting and the plain wood home for three coats of dark-blue acrylic paint.

"I can't possibly get to the health club by 9:30 to bicycle and meet my trainer at 10." "Remember what I told you about rushing," smiled my beautiful, stroke-hindered friend, Kathleen, as I dashed lipstick-less to the toilet. I was twenty minutes late for my workout. Afterwards, I ran to the framer and delivered the painted wood and the beautiful painting. When I got home, I looked at the pictures the committee had chosen for the show, and the painting wasn't on it. I now have a beautiful blue painting hanging over the dining room table in my home. P.S. In the end, they hung it in the show!

This is the *Dance of Our History*. It starts in the Garden of Eden, continues through Mount Sinai, the burning bush, slavery in Egypt, Jonah, Noah's Ark, the Old Testament, the Menorah, the Middle East, and the hand of God. Continuing clockwise is Eastern Europe and the Middle East. The scholar is studying Torah, the burning Shtetle, and the Holocaust. Below is the smuggling of Jews into Israel under the British "White Paper" and Jerusalem. In the lower corner is our rabbi behind the pulpit under the eternal light, with the choir by his side and the symbols of the Sabbath. Last is our temple, Temple Isaiah, as it looked in 1978, on the hill in front of the reservoir in Lafayette in the suburbs of San Francisco where I live. Helen Ann Licht 1978

Family Trip to Italy

"ITALIAN UN-RECONSTRUCTED!,", TUMBLED OUT OF my college son's mouth as he surveyed the large, run-down, rusticated, railroad station in Milan. As our slow-moving train came to a bumpy halt the doors opened. They expelled a mélange of people, dressed in Indian saris, jamas, robes, and all kinds of dress, There were punctured long haired hippies, enormous, flowery dressed women with brim-filled plastic bags, and sleek rushing men in business suits. All of them pushing through the almost impassable crowd as fast as they could.

The smokey haze around the disheveled expanse of low, grey, run-down wooden buildings near the tracks could have been fog. Open old horse-driven luggage carts, buskers, beggars and bums greeted us as we timidly ventured outside after the rush.

Jangling bells, sirens and the cacophony of the vibrant Italian peddlers drowned out our voices. We had to hang on to each other to keep from being separated. "Five hundred lira," screamed the gelato man as we passed. Rapid Italian language was a shock a first. The translation caught us completely unprepared. It was far too expensive.

We finally pushed our way back to the train. We shared a compartment with a darling couple from New York. They were sitting there slurping their cones. "Do you know how much those things cost?" my audacious son, Bruce, asked. The beautiful lady's face turned ashen. "Maybe we shouldn't be eating them." she exclaimed guiltily. We all laughed. She said her eighteen-year-old son would "never go to Europe with them." She was impressed. Bruce was a freshman at UCLA, Lisa, was thirteen. We had traveled all over the states, Hawaii, Mexico and Canada with our three children, but never to Europe.

My husband didn't like El Seguso. It was the pension on the Venetian Zattere where I had stayed two years before. "The beds are too hard." We shared one bathroom for the four of us and two meals were included. The view of the lighted Church of the Redentore across the Giudecca Canal didn't interest them as much as the gelato stand around the corner.

Bruce ran into a friend from high school on Piazza San Marco. He asked him to go to the Lido with him that night. We said, "Go," He decided to grouse around with us on the illuminated piazza eating gelato instead. I was flattered.

We sat on the steps of the Church of the Salute and watched the city lights across the canal. During our outside dinner with friends on top of the Hotel Danieli the waitress offered the children two desserts. Lisa was so excited. When she walked out of her stall in the restroom after dinner, two noisy, irritating, drunken ladies loudly exclaimed, "Oh, she's gorgeous!"

Florence partially worked. We spent seven days around the city. I had planned every minute. On the day we went to the Uffizi the children insisted on sitting in the lobby while my husband and I went through the galleries. The day I planned for the Church of San Lorenzo the family went shopping instead. We climbed the cathedral, saw the doors of Ghiberti, loved the Medici Chapel, the David and ate lots and lots and lots of gelato.

We took the train to Sienna for the famous Palio. Our seats were reserved in the center section. We had a wonderful lunch, saw the parade, visited with the contradi from each rival district, petted the costumed horses and ate Italian ice cream. Around four p.m. the clouds came in. Soaking wet and slurping gelato, we boarded the train back to Florence, tickets in hand. There was no way we could come back next year. I learned what they meant by a "rain check."

We took advantage of tours on the three days we were in Rome. We ran into so many people we knew from home in the Sistine Chapel that the guide finally told us, "We have fifteen minutes here, so you'd better stop talking and look." We did!

TRAVELS WITH AN ARTIST

We stayed in the small Internationale Hotel at the top of the Spanish Steps. The concierge told us the first time we were there, "another California family is staying here too." He left his desk and walked us down the street to a drugstore where they were eating lunch. We met them. They were from San Diego. They had two little children under three. Again, Norman and I went through the Borghese Gallery while the children happily stayed outside and bought T-shirts and gelato.

In the Blue Grotto we were serenaded by a toothless singer who didn't speak English. After Capri we returned to the Roman hotel and stayed in the young California family's vacated rooms. They had cherubs on the faded painted ceilings. There were no walls so we could walk all over the top of the small hotel. The huge room was unfinished and open to the hills behind and the view below. The best gelato was at the base of the steps.

We had a wonderful time with our children in Italy. They went back in later years and saw what they had missed.

Pontormo

O N A CAL EXTENSION ART history excursion in Florence a man in our class insisted, "You have to see the painting in the church of San Felicita!" The church was in a small cul de sac on the way to our class on the other side of the Arno River. Every day before nine a.m. we walked over the Ponte Vecchio past the site. The old church was always locked. Finally, one Friday morning the small wooden door was open.

We ran inside to see the huge painting on the front altar. It was a "Departure for the Tomb," by a sixteenth century artist named Pontormo. It showed the reclining Jesus, and weeping Mary in a central triangular pose. The colors were greyed out pinks, blues and browns with many emotional, elongated mannerist figures surrounding and holding them. It was awful! The painting was not our taste or interest at all. We hated it.

"I'll never remember this terrible painting," I said to myself as I begrudgingly began buying a postcard. "It's probably good for me to know it...like swallowing cod liver oil."

I walked into my studio when I arrived back in the states. There on the counter was my book on sixteenth century painting. It was too thick to take on our trip. On the cover was Pontormo's pink and blue, "Christ's Departure For the Tomb".

2021

Mexico City

I N MEXICO CITY DURING A fabulous family vacation, I met Gail. Gail was a cute, divorced American artist, living there with her two little boys. She had been married to a Mexican med student she met in college in Tucson, Arizona. He had become an ophthalmological surgeon in Mexico City and had a large, family who completely filled her life. When they were divorced, according to Mexican law she couldn't take her two young boys out of Mexico. She was living as an expatriate until they were grown.

Gail was a pretty, petite, energetic, freckle-faced cousin of my friend, Beverley Hillman. She took my children to see the mariachis in Plaza Garibaldi and invited me to a preview of her work at the *Instituto Mexicano Norte Americano De Relations Culturales* in the Zona Rosa. She asked me, "Why don't you show here too, in Mexico?" I thought about it. *Why not?* I applied to the gallery, and they offered me a show.

In March 1979, after I finished my degree in art history at Cal, I took ten canvases off their stretchers and rolled them up in my suitcase. I flew to Mexico City and built the stretchers there. Gail knew what to do.

I spent a month off and on in Mexico City, staying both with Gail and at the Hotel Genova in the Zona Rosa. Norman didn't come down for the preview. Gail and her teacher, Toby Joysmith, were there. The day of the show, I went around to all the commercial galleries in the Zona Rosa and left invitations. One gallery owner came. It was the Lanai Gallery. She took three of my paintings and placed them in a tennis club in Tepotzlan. The gallery owner sent me a money order for the sale. Americans weren't supposed to work in Mexico.

Gail showed me Mexico City. Along with her, I took three classes from Toby Joysmith, learning how to give my paintings an entirely new surface. He lived in a poor part of the city consisting of hundreds of lean-to houses and animals. This was a place I had never been. I loved being with her. We went out with many interesting American expatriates. John Gavin, a Stanford graduate, was the United States ambassador at the time.

At the Lagunilla market on Sundays we found all kinds of Mexican folk art. I bought two masks made of tin and interesting handmade jewelry. Gail showed me an altar designed by Vasarely, murals and mosaics, parks, antique shops, her friend's homes, and the exciting, cosmopolitan city like I had never seen it before. When she drove around the city, she would open the window of her little car and put her elbow out and make a fist at the terrible traffic blocking us from all sides, manipulating her way through the cacophony.

I loved Sundays at Chapultepec Park with the crowds, the spun sugar cones, the popcorn, barbecues, banners, and balloons. I even learned to hitchhike down the hill from Emperor Maximilion and Carlotta's rundown Chapultepec Castle. She introduced me to cajetta (goat's milk caramel), so much Mexican life, and the divergent, different neighborhoods of Mexico City.

On a European trip when the boys were in camp in 1977, Gail met Randy. He was a tall, handsome man, with wavy brown hair and a mustache, five years younger than Gail. He had finished his graduate work at Cornell. He was an assistant professor at what is now Pittsburgh University. They met in Paris and continued on to Greece. Once they met in the Midwest for a whitewater rafting trip. They were back at their separate homes when I met her. She showed me his picture when I stayed in Mexico with her. When his contract was up, he moved to Mexico City to be with Gail and the boys.

Gail was teaching art at the Jewish Community Center, a complex so large it encompassed athletic fields, theaters, tennis, dining, classrooms, and everything imaginable. I had never seen a place so crowded and immense.

Because Gail couldn't leave her children in Mexico, Randy took a job at the American School in Mexico City. They married. That led to more student tours to China, USSR, Eastern Europe, and Great Britain.

The boys grew up. Gail and Randy moved to Santa Fe and bought a charming adobe home. She furnished it with some of her large, wooden, Mexican antiques. I was with her when she bought them. Her colorful paintings and masks were on the wall. She bought an etching press, and Randy helped with the press. Gail supported herself by selling her beautiful prints and paintings. Randy was her printer, curator, and business manager. He also cooked.

They traveled to fine art shows all over the country every summer. Randy had a job for seven years at St. John's University teaching the classics. He was knowledgeable and charming. He gave backstage tours at the Santa Fe Opera, and together they ushered at the chamber music concerts in the beautiful, wooden concert hall at the city museum.

Going to the Santa Fe Opera with them was an experience. The tailgate was a grand picnic with a damask tablecloth, candles, wine, and a gourmet dinner prepared by chef Randy. One summer after Norman left Santa Fe, I stayed another week to take a printing course from her friend, Ron Pokrasso.

Unfortunately, we haven't been back to Santa Fe for years. I've seen Gail and Randy when they have come to San Francisco to participate in art shows. That, too, is almost over. Gail's boys are grown and married. They are having a terrific life in Santa Fe, teaching and sculpting. They were exciting friends at a wonderful time of my life.

Beautiful Buenos Aires

B EAUTIFUL BUENOS AIRES: WIDE STREETS, November's deep purple Jacaranda, palatial homes and green lawns surround elegant, sculpture-centered squares. Stylishly dressed, open-collared Portenos sun themselves in cafes across from stylish, short-skirted, smoking women. All is harmony.

The baby was left on the grandparents' doorsteps at midnight, with only a ring of the doorbell. There was not a word from the parents. Three weeks later, the grandparents received a call: "Uncle is coming to visit ... Have caviar, fine liquor, and leather goods for him." Three weeks later, another call ... a repeat. The third call came: "Uncle is not coming anymore." That night the parents were shot! The grandparents were lucky. They got to say Kaddish. "Disappeared" meant a person had vanished. One day they were there, the next day they were not. There was never a trace.

Embedded in the stones of the Plaza Mayor are mosaics of white bandanas, the symbols of the diapers their children wore when they were born. The Madres of the Plaza de Mayor wear them on their heads when they march every Thursday from three to five o'clock in front of the Casa Rosada, the "Pink Palace," where Evita once spoke. They still hoped for words of their sons and daughters, the "disappeared."

We were there with our rabbi, Roberto Graetz, marching in solidarity in 1995. It was an exciting city, a place we could love, but with a history that was hard to forget, like so many other places in our difficult, wonderful world.

Claudia Bernardi, an Argentine artist from San Francisco, is a member of the Forensic Society. She is one of the people called upon every time a mass grave is found. Her job is to help identify bones, dental charts, etc. as a means of informing the families. Some Argentine sites have been found, but it's a long process before many of the other families can say, Kaddish.

December 4, 1999

History of London through its Architecture

WE SPENT FOUR WEEKS IN a dorm in London, a brutalist, gray, cement building at the Royal College of Art. It was 1985, and my husband, Norman, had recently retired. Our plain, small upstairs room had barely space for a queen-size bed, a desk, and an open closet. We were given three keys: one to the dorm entrance, one to our room, and one to the shared bathroom across the hall.

The spare dining room was where we met our dorm mates. Most were young, with a sprinkling of people our age, mostly gray-haired couples, the "wrinklies," taking classes for the summer. It was quite a change from the luxurious hotels like the Mauna Kea in Hawaii and the Peninsula in Hong Kong, where we stayed when my husband was in business. We found that we liked it.

The dorm was directly behind the Victoria and Albert Museum, "the V and A," as it was fondly called, and a block from Albert Hall, a round, red-brick Victorian building modeled after a Roman amphitheater. The summer popular musical, "Proms," was held there every Sunday night.

We were between the charming park, Kensington Gardens, with its spired and mosaicked mid-Victorian memorial statue of Prince Albert, Queen Victoria's husband, and a cute district of inexpensive ethnic restaurants, boutiques, and raucous, screaming stands of telltale tabloids.

The class we took, "The History of London through Its Architecture," was given by UCLA Extension. We went from the Roman wall to Sir Richard Roger's modernist building, Lloyd's of London. (Docklands had yet to be built.) Not only did we tour the entire city, we studied the history, the buildings, and the neighborhoods. Architects included Inigo Jones, Christopher Wren, John Gibbs, the Adams brothers, John Nash, Nicholas Hawksmoor, and many more.

We visited samples of Tudor, Renaissance, Regency, Restoration, Victorian, and Georgian buildings, with excursions to Bath, Ely Cathedral, and Cambridge. We even went to Greenwich to see Wren's Royal Naval College. On a free weekend Norman and I took the train to Brighton to see John Nash's Royal Pavilion, with its bulbous domes designed for crazy King George.

Our friends, Marty and Carol, came to London for a few days and stayed near us. When they arrived, Marty came to our dorm. He had to ask a student to take him through the corridors and up the stairs to find us, as we had no phone. To call outside we had to find a red, glass phone booth and use a telephone card.

Carol wanted to go on the Orient Express. We caught it early one Saturday morning at Victoria Station and spent a day riding in softly rattling luxury to Dover and back with a stop for lunch at Ann Boleyn's family castle. In the dining room were hanging large ancestor portraits. Suits of armor lined the walls. Marty was having a problem with our temple back home, and that was all he talked about at the large wooden table where we were eating, among memories of knights and elegant and tragic English history.

Afternoon tea was served by a tuxedo-clad butler in our private compartment. The old-fashioned steel train rambled on to London via the beautiful English countryside. It was a sample of the famous elegant train ride that has been written about in so much literature. Fortunately, there was no murder.

Glyndebourne

F RIENDS WHO HAD LIVED IN London alerted us to Glyndebourne, the famous black-tie summer opera festival in Leeds. We were lucky to get tickets. I had ordered them many months before. We were seated in the last row of the balcony.

Norman refused to rent a tuxedo. He brought his tuxedo from home. As he went to claim the tickets downstairs in the only dormitory safe, one of the students asked him if he was a waiter. I wore a washable long black skirt, traveling clothes.

We took the bus to Victoria Station. There we saw a group in formal dress and joined them as we boarded the train. We sat with a couple our age from Washington, D.C. who invited us to tea during intermission. A bus met the arrivals at the train station in Leeds.

When we reached Glyndebourne, we walked among the tuxedoed throngs picnicking on blankets on the grass among the sheep. They had decorated baskets full of gourmet food, table cloths, candles, and wine specially ordered from the fancy food courts of Harrods.

Norman had refused to picnic in his tux. We ate in the Lower Wallop, where Norm had made a reservation and ordered sliced, smoked salmon, which was waiting for us at our table as we sat down. After the salmon we lined up for the sumptuous buffet supper. The couple we met on the train were eating their dinner in the high-end Upper Wallop.

After dinner and another leisurely stroll through the picnickers, a bell rang, and we were escorted through the magnificent manor house. We admired the paintings and treasures on our way to our top, last-row seats in the small, connected opera house to see Janacek's opera, *Katya Kabanova*. The singer's red hair, ultramarine blue dress, and lounging pose against a stark emerald green hill and blue sky reminded me of *Christina's World*, by Andrew Wyeth, but the set was much brighter than the painting.

We were lucky to see the same opera with the same set at the new opera house in Paris a few years later. This site was about five times larger. We read that Glyndebourne is much larger now and more famous. I'm happy we saw it when it was smaller and more intimate.

The British Museum

ONCE I WENT ON A tour with the Stanford classics department to the British Museum. We handled Babylonian stone tablets that were used for ordering laundry and other household chores. We even visited the working laboratory. I had toured the museum once before on a short highlights tour. Despite being in the museum for ten days, we barely touched the surface.

I was on the second part of the classics tour. Our leader, Patrick Hunt, was very knowledgeable. He told us that If we would be willing to skip lunch, he would take us through the Elgin marbles, the lion hunt, and the Egyptian section that we had missed. One of my favorite parts was the Sumerian section. I saw the little rams from Ur again and again. I even saw them when they went to the Met in New York.

Wandering the museum alone, I came upon the Mildenhall Treasure, the spectacular Roman silver service that was ploughed up in the hills of Suffolk in 1942. I had seen a fast slide of it in an Orinda art history class before the trip, but I had barely paid attention. Recognizing it by accident and seeing the pagan-Christian iconography from the fourth century was so exciting. I loved the leg shields (grieves), which were written about in the Iliad. I also learned to appreciate the Greek vases.

When the class was over, I paid to see the extra exhibit on Lord Hamilton in the museum. I wanted to see George Romney's paintings of Emma. As I walked out, I was met at the door by our instructor, Patrick Hunt, who said, "You mean you went into that exhibit without me?"

He marched me right back in and told me about Hamilton's excavations on Mount Vesuvius and his designs for Wedgewood. I loved Hamilton's story about his *menage a' trois* with Emma and Admiral Lord Nelson. It was so well told in *The Volcano Lovers*, by Susan Sontag.

I'll always love London, and I have returned many times, for as Samuel Johnson famously said, "When a man is tired of London, he's tired of life."

Travels with an Artist

"TRAVELS WITH AN ARTIST" WAS my byline. Without a copyright, it carried me through the years. It started when I sat beside a travel agent at a party. I mentioned I had a friend who led tours in Paris. I really wanted to go. She told me, "I'll use you as an escort, not your friend." I was off. I planned a one-week tour of Paris, four days in the city and three in the chateaux country and Mount Michel. People signed up.

I didn't know what to do.: one couple almost missed the plane. *Should I get on with the tour or stay and wait for them at the airport?* They arrived as the plane was loading, and I pushed them through. (It was really frightening, but I learned that you get on with the tour.) They would have had to take the terrible consequences.

We had a skilled, knowledgeable guide. I didn't plan to go to Omaha Beach, since ours was an art tour, not a history tour. The French facilitator put it on the itinerary, and one person insisted. We reluctantly went—yet it was one of the best parts. Because of that, we had to have a midnight cocktail party on the bus back to Paris. Nobody complained.

I bailed someone out of the Follies Bergere at 3:00 a.m. On a tour through Champagne country, we had an interminable lunch. Course after course came, and I didn't know how to stop it. Everyone loved it. Rheims Cathedral closed to tourists at five, and I was worried we would miss it. We barely made it in time. Once we were caught in a strike and had to carry our own suitcases across the railroad tracks. Again, nobody complained. We saw everything I wanted to see all around Paris.

My husband and some friends came on one of the tours. My last French tour to Paris and the Riviera turned out to be all women. My husband was going, but he copped out. When he retired, we were lucky to go again and again and stay longer.

I lectured on Paris at the Orinda Community Center. I had a hard time with French, even though I had taken a class. I had to pronounce the French words in English as my pronunciation was so poor. *Tromp d'oil* (?) and *Chinoserie* became "fool the eye" and "Chinese style." Still, "Travels with an artist" went on.

Deux Continents

I T WAS PARIS! IT WAS France! It was so long ago. The ancient city of Napoleon was full of passages, carousels, and twentieth century art! My husband, Norman, and I were on a University of California Extension tour through Paris, Provence, and the Riviera in 1976. It started with a week in Montmartre. There was even a daylight murder across the street from our hotel.

On the bus to the Riviera, my husband befriended a troubled, beautiful woman. Louise was a tall, longhaired, blond woman of indeterminate age, separated but not divorced from the socialite scion of an important multi-generational family in St. Paul, Minnesota. The family ran a fancy store that was similar to London's famous Fortnum and Mason, with expensive merchandise like gourmet jams, exotic candies, beautiful cashmere blankets, and luxury clothing. My friend, Rhoda, had offered to show it to me when I visited her in St. Paul three years before. It was one of the must-see places. Louise's husband was the son of this wealthy family. They had six or seven kids. She planned to divorce him. After the divorce, she was planning on traveling all over Europe.

She was a tennis player and a former Miss Minnesota. My husband, also a tennis player, visited with her constantly on the bus from Paris, through Provence, the Riviera, and back to Paris. We invited her visit us to try out the tennis courts in California.

After the tour, we were both signed up for second Cal extension classes: she for the London theater class and I to study the Bel Epoch in Paris. We both had a free week in Paris in between. Norman stayed there with me. Jonathan, her darling, divorced boyfriend, came to Paris for the week. He was a handsome, ex-congressman from Nebraska with two grown kids and a constant smile. He was so excited to be in Paris for the first time and very much in love with her.

They stayed in a small walk-up room on the top floor of the small Hotel des Deux Continents on the charming Rue Jacob. We stayed at the old Bonapart Hotel, a few blocks away, both in the charming sixth arrondissement neighborhood of St. Germain des Pres.

We met each night at ten for a drink at the Cafe Deux Maggot, the cafe frequented by Picasso and his friends. Picasso's small, stark, stone statue was in the courtyard of the church of St. Germain des Pres across the street. It was commissioned in homage to his friend, the poet, Apollinaire. It was rumored it was a portrait of his mistress, Dora Mar, recycled.

Louise stood in line at the Paris opera house, the Palais Garnier, to buy four tickets in the king's box for us to attend the Paris ballet. We brought hors d'oeuvres and she, the wine. We loved sitting below the crystal chandelier, pink and blue dancers and musicians on the painted Mark Chagall ceiling, as the fat wealthy bankers and their Belle Epoch mistresses had at the turn of the century.

We were home for six weeks when I received a call. Louise and Jonathan had attended a family wedding in St. Paul. Her estranged husband had invited them to her former home on the lake for a drink after the wedding and shot them! Rhoda sent me the papers about the sensational crime. Louise's husband was from a prominent, wealthy family, so he got off with insanity. What a shock!

Norman and I now stay at the Hotel des Deux Continents in the romantic top floor walkup, the small room with the balcony full of geraniums, overlooking the rooftops of Paris.

Belle Epoque

W E LIVED BESIDE THE BOIS de Boulogne, a wild rambling park where ladies of the night wandered, waiting for a pickup, when I took the next Cal extension class in the Belle Epoch. The area of our dorm was famous for the first small model of the Statue of Liberty, the Villa la Roche by Le Corbusier and many neglected Belle Epoch homes.

Our professor was a musician. We learned about Ravel, Du Parc, Faure', Satie, and other turn-of-the-century composers. Oscar Wilde, Manet, Whistler, and Courbet were among the artists discussed. I had thought I was tired of the Museum Orsay, but after revisiting it with the class, I went back many times.

On our morning excursion to the Palace Garnier, the opera house designed for Napoleon III, we toured from the roof to the basement. We saw the underground water and the ladder that must have inspired *The Phantom of the Opera*. My friends and I took hard-boiled eggs from breakfast that day and ate them in the restroom of the Cordon Bleu before watching an afternoon gourmet cooking class We listened to an English translator. Afterward, we tasted the fabulous food.

Sharon, my California friend, lived in the room next door. We went to lunch after class one day at the Tour d'Argent. Our husbands never took us there. Dressed in high heels, we boarded a chintz-wallpapered elevator and emerged to an empty room with a wide window. We felt we were sitting on top of Notre Dame. Only one Japanese couple was eating lunch when we were there. We loved it so much I bought a souvenir Limoges box with a picture.

Our high heels stopped our sightseeing for the rest of the day. Now the restaurant is gone, and Notre Dame was destroyed by fire.

I was invited to visit Chartres with three women for Bastille Day, but I had a date with Sharon. I told my friend, "I've been there twice." She answered, "I've been there seven times." I was very sorry I didn't go. Sharon would have gone too, if I had asked her in time. We spent a restful day in the Park Monceau instead. We really needed it. Afterwards we wandered through the firecrackers and concessions by the Seine.

I have never found the little cafes and bookshops we discovered on that trip again. Walking by the old Pre Catalan in the Bois de Boulogne with a friend, seeing the outdoor diners, I mentioned, "I remember being there with friends on a rainy night many years ago." She said, "You are so lucky." I know I am. I returned to the restaurant with Norman on my last trip to Paris. It was an elegant experience I'll never forget.

Café

BOULEVARD ST. GERMAIN AND RUE Bonaparte meet in front of Café Deux Magots. Back to back, dressed in celadon robes and coolie hats, two bearded, wooden Chinese commercial agents (magots) sit on pillars presiding over the smoke-filled room. I imagined John Paul Sartre, Simone de Beauvoir, Hemingway, and Picasso inside the inside dark room discussing philosophy and the intellectual life of Paris in the 1920s. Across the street from the café was the churchyard of St-Germain-des-Pres with the Picasso statue of Apollinaire.

During a class in Paris, I befriended a charismatic lady in her fifties. She had long gray hair and wore cut-off jeans every day. During one of our after-class explorations we stopped by the outside café with two other ladies. The waiter seated us in a hidden table in the back. This was the lament of many single ladies visiting Paris restaurants.

Norman and I often sat at a front table drinking our expensive coffee and visiting with the stylish Parisians and tourists. We even went there for dinner on our last night in Paris in 2000, and we were seated next to some people from the California town where we live.

The eighteenth-century Wallace drinking fountain next door was still there, and the back room had a new coat of paint. But a new restaurant had been built in front of the café, obscuring the beautiful view of the church square with the statue of Apollinaire. As author Thomas Wolfe once said, "You can't go home again."

Graffiti

"**G**RAFFITI'S THE ART OF THE '90s," my photography instructor, Ron Zak, said. "I can't believe that," I countered. He was so right. It's the art of the '90s, the twentieth and the twenty-first centuries—and how long it will go on, nobody knows.

I was in Paris in 1990 on a photography tour from Napa Valley College. I chose it because it was cheap. I didn't appreciate it at the time, because I was the oldest in the diverse group. I didn't go to the pre-trip meeting. I shared no interests with the young students. As the eldest, I thought they might respect my worldly knowledge, but they didn't. Some of the girls shopped for lacy underwear to wear for their boyfriends back home, and some didn't even speak good English. They had no interest in art. What a wonderful introduction to another part of the world for them.

We stayed in an upstairs pension between the Luxembourg Gardens and the Church of St-Sulpice. It was a perfect spot for walking and riding the bus with our monthly pass past all the monuments. I learned where to stop to rest with only a black coffee. My favorite daily lunch was a ham sandwich on a French roll. I lugged a large camera with many lenses.

Ron would drop us off at places like Pere Lachaise Cemetery with our hard-boiled egg and extra breakfast toast, and we'd photograph for the whole day. My shots were not great, and I was lonely in the vast, cool cemetery, but I learned to know it well. Oscar Wilde, Chopin, and Jim Morrison of The Doors kept me busy.

My favorite spot was Trocadero, where I kneeled on the wide, central cement plaza and photographed skate boarders looking like they were jumping over the Eiffel Tower. It was located beside the river, just below the hill, and was quite a backdrop. Even if the photos were blurry, I used them for years as the subjects of my paintings. I even showed some of these blurred photos in a winery in Napa in one of Ron's shows.

We spent time in the passages and lower Montmartre photographing the carousel, the stairs, and the Abbesses Belle Epoch subway station. We photographed bridges, buildings, door knobs, and sculpture. We went to no museums, and I missed the concerts in the churches. Nobody in our group was interested.

A young school teacher I met at the pension wanted to hear them too. I went with him. I loved studying the interiors of the grand cathedrals and listening to classical music at the same time. I even spent Bastille Day walking around with him. After lunch there were firecrackers around the Eiffel Tower. I spent another day by myself, studying the domes of four grand cathedrals, traveling with my bus pass to many different neighborhoods.

Ron had a sharp sense of humor. But I didn't relate to him at all. He met my husband after the trip, and they bonded with great repartee. Ron and the people in the class continued to photograph together around San Francisco and to show their photos in the wine country. Some of the photography people came to my art shows after the tour, and we kept in touch for years. I learned so much. Paris was very affordable, and the trip enabled me to know it well.

China Remembered

THE WHITE LACE CURTAINS COVERED the windows and obliterated the landscape as the BART-like train jangled across the border into China. It was May 1987. I was escorting a tour of five women to a country that recently opened to the West. Waiting for the train was difficult. We got up early and were marooned in a station where nobody spoke English. After immigration procedures, we waited. Finally, the train left at 10:00 a.m. We ran to catch it with barely minutes to spare. Our seats were reserved. The bland wooden seats bumped us awake as we rode. We bought dried mango and wax-paper-wrapped chicken legs on the train. We were so hungry, and they were so good.

I was fighting a sneezy, runny cold, having caught it at the bar at the top of the Mandarin Hotel in Hong Kong the night before. I had invited the women for drinks and forgotten to warn them of the frigid air conditioning after the steaming heat of the city. I was the only one sick on the train. I was really worried that my cough would spoil my trip. Two of the ladies bought me a bottle of cognac, which helped.

After leaving a long dark tunnel, we rumbled through the new territories of Hong Kong. The hills in the distance were covered with dense vegetation that made them look like Hawaii. Some hills looked as though orange nasturtiums were running down the slopes.

The new buildings under construction were trussed with bamboo. High-rise apartments ringed the flat, cultivated fields. Some fields had what looked like modern dams in the streams around them. There were farmers' rest houses in the middle of the fields, with sloping, colored temple-like structures on top. Barefoot workers wore bamboo hats and carried their wrapped, hanging loads balanced by a bamboo pole across their bent shoulders. Three long, crossed bamboo poles served as the site markers at the confluence of every field. They were in the shape of American Indian tipis.

The highways and bridges were modern. We passed small towns, waterfront tree-lined roads, little islands that poked up all around, and men rowing junks on the water. There was always a highway between the train and the water.

Canton (Guangzhou)

WHEN WE CROSSED THE BORDER into China, the landscape changed. It was not as modern or kept up. When we arrived at the old Victorian Station in Guangzhou (Canton), it was 1:00 p.m. I was coughing and sneezing and in terrible shape. The uniformed young lady who greeted us said to me, "Don't worry." She took me to an apothecary, who mixed me a hot herbal medicine drink that kept me well for the rest of the trip.

It had been a long time since the 1930s Long March. The Nationalist Kuomintang party exited China, taking much of its movable art to Formosa. Under Mao Zedong, Communist China had been closed to most of the outside world until President Richard Nixon visited in 1972. Diplomatic relations with the United States were finalized in 1979.

In the huge thirty-five passenger bus that met us, the five of us were lost. The paved, tree-lined road into Guangzhou was crowded with bicyclists. The people wore brown clothes with round, woven, brown, peaked hats. Occasionally an old car appeared. Palms and other spindly trees lined the side of the road.

Our guide pointed out two tall cement buildings in the Brutalist style. They were out of place at the time, with flat land all around them. They were the first of new housing built under Chairman Mao to serve China's enormous population. She explained that two or three families could occupy one small apartment with up to two rooms, a kitchen, and a real bathroom. They were the lucky ones, as the places where ordinary people lived were very rundown. There were so many people in line for them that they had to have a lottery.

We were told we were not to tip the guides, but we could offer something, perhaps two or three dollars, but "not in front of officials." We were also told to buy stamps if we could find them in Canton, as they were in short supply all over China.

I hardly remember Canton. It seemed very flat, busy, and unplanned, with hawkers selling scrolls of flower paintings and other cheap articles. It was full of bicycles everywhere and was very quiet.

I remember the Sun Yat-Sen complex, a large, faded, octagonal building with wooden, backless stadium seats and dust all over. Sun Yat-Sen was the first leader of the Nationalist Party. He was memorialized but not revered by the Communists.

We saw a temple, a jade and ivory factory, a cultural park, and pickled fish. Then we had a beautiful nine-course dinner in a private room above a bakery. It consisted of winter melon soup, a shredded chow mein-like vegetable on straw noodles, additional vegetables, pea shoots and mushrooms, ginger beef, dim sum shrimp, plum pot stickers, eggrolls, cookies, and pineapple. We were not allowed to eat with the local people.

Canton reminded me of Benares, India, at rush hour. There were so many people walking and so many peddlers; only the signage was Chinese.

Guilin

W E FLEW TO GUILIN, A four-hour flight followed by a hot three-hour drive. We seemed to be the only English-speaking people in the airport, and the five of us were alone. We were really scared and unprepared. The airport was a huge, plain, crowded room with only one little old lady sweeping the entire floor. The flight time announcements were noisily flipping on the boards. We couldn't understand them at all. Every time a plane would leave or arrive, an announcement would strike out loudly in Chinese. Lights would blink, and a buzzer would sound. We always jumped. It reminded us of a casino in Las Vegas, but the language was Chinese. We were confused and frightened that we would miss our plane, until we met a jovial, bearded, heavyset man and his wife from America, who cradled a large, garish, green, pottery Buddha in his arms. He was so friendly and helpful because he had been there before, but he was gauche, and we were grateful he wasn't on our tour. He interpreted for us. The plane to Guilin left at 9:45 p.m., one half hour late.

Guilin is a city on the Li River surrounded by small, pointed limestone mountains called karsts. The old art deco Li River Hotel was across from the low, cement-fenced, Chinese-style, river walk. It was a frustrating stay as our guide, Yuan, was very intense. It was hard for us to understand her English. She greeted us by saying she was to meet "five old ladies" and gave us a canned talk on Guilin. She left us alone at the hotel.

The hotel was not as bad as we expected. The view from the large picture window was like a sixteenth-century Chinese ink and silk landscape scroll with mountains behind the river. The only thing missing was the old philosopher in the lower left-hand corner. The furnishings in the room were old and brown.

In the morning we could look out the window and see people doing tai chi in a pavilion by the water. The Li River was full of cormorants. The long-necked gray and white birds had tight bands around their necks so they could fish for the men in the low, barge-like boats. The fishermen grabbed the fish from the cormorants' long, pointed beaks because the birds could not swallow them. We felt this was really mean.

The next day the gruff guide rushed us to a boat. We were late, and a Chinese family was already sitting at our table. My friend, Lorna, made friends with the family. We had lunch together in spite of their lack of English. They were a bride and groom and a mother. Lorna was invited to their home in Xi'an. The only catch was, they wouldn't be home when we were there.

On the boat trip, we passed one beautiful, pointed mountain after another. I bought a carved chop. "The only one," my peddler said. My friend, Bev, was sad that she didn't get one. The vender went to the bottom of the pile in his box and found an even more beautiful one for her. We learned to search the bottom of the boxes for everything we bought.

A sudden rain soaked us, but the low humidity dried us out fast. When we landed, our guide quickly rushed us past all the cheap souvenir stands. We didn't have any money anyway. We had arrived in Guilin after the banks were closed for the weekend, and we left Monday before they opened.

We were not allowed to mix with the people. We ate separately. We saw where the people ate. All the tables were covered with dirty dishes. They didn't clean them for hours. Lorna and I sneaked out to the people's latrines, and we found about ten flat, standup, dirty latrines, all in a row with no privacy. They were like the latrines in Ephesus and in Auschwitz, except they were flat in the ground. We had been told to wear skirts all through China, as standing was the only way to do your stuff. There was only one small, cold-water faucet for washing hands.

TRAVELS WITH AN ARTIST

We loved seeing the white and purple lotus growing out of the swamps and the green rice fields cultivated by stooped, blue-clad women and men wearing coolie hats. They had to manipulate hand plows. It saddened us to see poor people working so hard. Again, there were very few cars, many bicycles. The roads were not finished, and there were big boulders in the middle in some places. We saw a school decorated for Children's Day. It had paper butterflies on the outside walls. The only children we saw had big bows and rouge on their faces. Our guide wouldn't let us visit.

The driver left to have his car repaired, and we had to wait for him to return. Our guide tried over and over again to take us to the Friendship Store, but we avoided her every try. At the zoo, unfortunately, the one panda was sick, so we couldn't see him. The women in our group bought panda t-shirts at an outdoor stand. We toured the Reed Flute Cave, climbing many stories deep inside. It was lit up, cheesy, and crowded with Japanese tourists. I was glad I was not a spelunker, but after the cave and the boat trip, there was nothing else to do in Guilin.

There was no airline schedule, and our plane didn't arrive for over a day and a half. Our rigid guide wouldn't let us walk out alone, day or night. She said, "Too dangerous." We walked anyway. It really upset our unbendable guide. I thought I'd have a rebellion of the women on my hands. I remember two beautiful, large, flowered cloisonné bowls in the hotel gift shop. We couldn't buy them. Either they were not for sale or we couldn't carry them. Finally, after a day and a half of boring waiting, our plane arrived.

Xi'an (Siam)

THE UNDERGROUND ARMY WAS ONLY partially excavated in the open air. It was covered with a corrugated tin roof. We walked around the raised, wooden platform encircling the large pit in Xi'an. We saw about twenty of the famous life-size statues ten feet below. People were smaller at that time. Each sculpture was individualized. The rest of the site was unexcavated rubble. You could only climb around them if you were an official.

A group of farmers had discovered the tomb while ploughing a field around 1917. The famous Emperor Qin Shi Huang Ti was buried there around 210 B.C. with his live servants, horses, concubines, and hundreds of lifelike statues. He famously burned all the history books in 213 B.C. Much of China's ancient history was lost. He united China as the emperor of the Qin Dynasty.

I was overwhelmed when I was first told about the many small, round hills in China that had not yet been excavated. There aren't enough archeological teams to do the specialized job of archiving and preserving the artifacts so they don't disintegrate when they arrive in the open air. If tomb robbers discovered a grave, they would rob it of its contents and sell it to unscrupulous antique dealers all over the world. Heads were broken off and separated from bodies. The artifacts weren't catalogued. People didn't realize that these were sacred statues. Collectors and dealers had no regard for the ancient religions. Fortunately, that has changed.

Neolithic Ban Po pottery, some of the earliest decorated artifacts from 6,000 years ago, was discovered in X'ian also. Post holes were discovered. The bones of ancient children were buried in large pots.

One fact that I will always remember is that the city of Washington, D.C., was partially modeled on the famous plan of old Chang'an (Xi'an). X'ian was an interesting, dirty city with a mysterious Muslim quarter. Another name for the city was Sian. It served as the eastern entrance to the Silk Road in the seventeenth-century Tang Dynasty.

We visited and observed the Ming Dynasty city wall, the Great Mosque, the Drum Tower complete with a drum concert, the golden chariot, and Neolithic tools found in many of the ancient sites. Lorna and I climbed three stories of the Wild Goose Pagoda.

The Muslim quarter had wonderful food. There were Tang dancers to entertain us at the Old People's Hotel. We sat in the second row and could savor the costumes and instruments. We loved the masked dance and the drum dance. It seemed really authentic, with young local dancers and musicians.

I had researched a little folk-art store before the trip. There, I bought a gorgeous black, minority-crafted coat embroidered with red roses. It was too small for me, as the people were little. I had it altered into an evening coat when I arrived home. I'm sure it lost much of its value. Of the minority work I have collected from all over the world, some of the best was in X'ian at that time. The city was exotic and very exciting.

Beijing

BEFORE WE FLEW TO BEIJING, we waited in the Xi'an airport again for three hours. There, we visited with a Guatemalan opera singer and her husband, who was a descendent of Simon Bolivar. We talked about Guatemalan textiles. Meeting interesting people from all over the world was a great bonus on our trip.

We arrived at the modern airport In Beijing. It was built in 1980. The wide road into the city was lined with double rows of trees, leafy green and sprouting on the outside and willows on the inside. We passed through the imposing city gates.

On the drive into town, we passed an observatory building with large solar instruments on top of the tower gate, a large lake with boats at the Lungwhen Pagoda, and a street of antiques in closed, Chinese-style buildings that looked touristy. Beijing already had many new apartments like the two we saw in Guangzhou. They were by the river. One after another, they looked like redevelopment, gray or faded green or pink. They rose very high and were numbered 1, 2, 3, 4, 5, 6, etc. in large black letters. The government was in charge of collecting the rents. Policemen in white uniforms stood in the circles in the center of the roads.

We passed dingy lean-to stores with old men sitting before them. Children were playing games among the street stands. There were lots of army uniforms and Mao caps. We passed Tiananmen Square, with a huge red tablet and the reviewing stand in front of the congress building. After we had a Peking duck dinner, Bev and I walked down the street by ourselves, looking around. Nobody else spoke English.

On the Great Wall, we found ourselves walking among people from all over the world. Men in colorful turbans, women in saris, people in traditional African robes, and men in sheepskin were climbing up the steep passage with us from the first large turret to the next. It was a slow, silent, procession. So many languages were spoken, but we never heard English. There were no peddlers. By overlooking the shoulder-high crenelated walls, we could see a small village located deep in the valley.

I will never forget that first trip to the Great Wall. On my visit with Norman twenty years later, it had changed so much. There were so many Americans. It had lots of tourist shops at the base, with signs in English. Seated, persistent, peddlers were located every few feet of the climb, hawking cheap souvenirs.

The next day we visited Tiananmen Square. It was crowded. There was a huge line to see Mao's Tomb. There were big Russian-style buildings at the edge, with a prominent picture of Mao in the center. We went there again at night, and it was nearly empty except for a few cute, Chinese young people wanting to take our picture.

I hardly remember the Imperial City. It was dusty, disheveled, dark, and large. We could only see through a dirty window where the Chin emperor lived. We saw cloisonné, ceramics, mahogany chairs, and thrones. I remember the magnificent stone lion carvings at the entrance and the waterless stone waterfall. Later, we went to the Clock Museum and the Jewelry Museum. The buildings were recently renovated and were edged with bright green and red ceramics called nine-dragon tiles. A snapping dragon leaped out of each corner roof.

That afternoon we went to the Summer Palace. We only saw it from a distance as a pavilion on top of the hill, but the lake in front was full of people sailing dragon-headed boats. There was even a carved stone boat on the side of the lake. It was a long, beautiful walk with carved stonework fences on the sides. We really enjoyed it, even though it was very crowded. The full bus parking lot was huge. My friend, Beverley, got lost among the forty or fifty buses. Before we found her, she was really disoriented and scared. Nobody else spoke English.

The animal and guardian carvings at the Ming Tombs were lovely, but the tombs we saw were empty and not worth it. I heard that some were painted inside—we didn't see them. They had barrel vaulting and inside stairs. Of the thirteen tombs, only two were open. There were good souvenirs outside the tombs, but our guide vehemently discouraged us from buying them, as she said they were "too expensive." We were hot and tired when we returned for dinner at another restaurant with Silk Road dancers. We found them very touristy after enjoying the local dancers in Sian.

After dinner, the five of us went by taxi to the Great Wall Hotel for Mai Tai on the roof. The hotel was designed by John Portman, the architect who designed the Embarcadero Center in San Francisco. It was a long way out of town. It had beautiful ivory carvings and vases in the lobby. In the gift shop was a little Chinese opera doll I didn't have time to buy, and I was really sorry. The face was a mask. It had long feathers and patterns and big flags in back. It was around finger height. I sadly drew a picture of it. Back in the states the women suggested I send for it. I did, one for me and one for Lisa. I sent the picture describing the doll to the hotel, and the dolls arrived very quickly. There was a handwritten note inside asking me to write back to them to tell them how I liked them. I wrote back to them and told them, I liked them very much.

We went to the zoo and saw a panda and its baby. Then we went on to the Temple of Heaven. It was a big, painted wooden compound consisting of three buildings. We were only allowed to look into the larger one. It was very high, round, and complex, painted in reds, blues, and greens, bright Chinese colors. After a Peking duck dinner, we left Beijing.

Shanghai

THE LAST CITY WE VISITED was Shanghai, the old city on the Huang Po River. The big bus let us out on the Bund. These were the dusty, dilapidated art deco buildings used by the foreign traders from the 1860s to the 1930s. The guide suggested we stop on Nanjing Road at the flat grassy park on the river side and talk to the men who were sitting around wanting to talk to us to practice their English. They asked us about San Francisco and Dianne Feinstein. This was our first real contact with the Chinese people. We visited on the flat green area, at the same level as the river. The dirty river was filled with gray tug boats, barges, oil tankers and other industrial ships. We couldn't see the other side, as all the dingy boats were blocking it. We heard it consisted of fields for farming.

Lorna and I tried to find the Jewish quarter, but nobody knew where it was. I bought an embroidered black-petaled minority dance skirt at the very end of the third Russian-style building of the Friendship Store in the French Quarter—thanks to my book, *Shopping in China*.

I also bought some Chinese ink in a small, round ceramic box that had a beautiful, blue landscape painting on it. I didn't look inside the closed box when they handed it to me. The painting turned out to be black when I opened it at home; I learned to open closed boxes before I accept them. We also visited a chanting service in the Jade Buddha Temple and saw a beautiful, carved Wei Dynasty stone sculpture in a case, along with other antiques.

My friend, Pam, who grew up in Shanghai during the war, told us many stories about it. She wanted us to see her church. She told us it was painted black when her family left. I asked the guide to show it to us. She insisted, "There is no black church in Shanghai." I was walking through the third floor by an open window of the old wooden Shanghai museum when I looked out, and there it was, black steeple and all. When I next returned to China many years later, everything had changed. There was no church and a new museum. When my tour left Shanghai, my cold returned in all its fury.

Dave Wong

DAVE WONG WAS ONE OF the editors of the *Stanford Daily* when I was a copywriter in 1952. I vaguely remember a Chinese dinner in an underground San Francisco restaurant with Dave and some of his friends. When my husband started to do business in Hong Kong, I looked up Dave. He was the managing director of an international trading company, and he had a race horse in a place called Happy Valley. We met at the Peninsula Hotel.

Norman and I enjoyed Dave's company so much. He would take us to English-style restaurants in Hong Kong, when all we wanted to do was eat the local Chinese food. In 1984 Dave married a beautiful young girl from a city called Nantong in China. It was difficult for him—he was questioned in public by people wanting to know why they wanted to get married, since he was 35 years older. He had to go before the town council to take her away from China. He bought her family an apartment after they were married.

When Dave married Zhao Jie 赵洁 and brought her to Hong Kong, we met for lunch at a hotel on Chinese New Year. Kitty, as he called her, didn't speak English. As Dave and Norman rattled away about business and international politics, Kitty offered to take me shopping.

When Dave and Kitty visited San Francisco, we took them to an Italian restaurant in North Beach. The next day we met them at the BART station when they came to our home. He wore a cute red Stanford sweatshirt. I served him a cottage cheese lunch. But he didn't like cottage cheese.

In Hong Kong, on the way home from my first tour of China in 1989, he took me to a steak restaurant for lunch. Before China took over Hong Kong in 1997, Dave and Kitty had moved to London. Kitty wanted to learn English, and Dave wanted peace and quiet to write. We visited London too. We would meet at a metro stop in Piccadilly Circus. We enjoyed London's nearby Chinatown restaurants with them several times, although nobody there spoke English. Dave ordered for us.

Kitty developed into a stylish, sophisticated woman, and Dave followed his dream of being a writer. I have many of his books of Hong Kong history and short stories. Many of his stories were broadcast by the BBC and radio stations all over Europe. He was also published in magazines all over Europe.

Kitty was a wonderful cook and enjoyed the life in London. They grew separate, and eventually parted. Kitty went back to China, and Dave moved to Kuala Lumpur to continue his writing. When I last heard from Kitty, she was single. She works for a charity that has helped more than 5,000 children go to school. She sent me a picture of the darling children she was teaching. She said she is very happy.

I felt sad about Dave. I had barely heard about Kuala Lumpur, and I knew I would never get there. I could hardly believe it when I received an e-mail from my grandson, Wyatt. He had been traveling and working in Asia. He was in Kuala Lumpur. He had tea with Dave. Dave was old, and he had just published another book. Dave gave him his book. What a treat for me to hear about it!

Hanoi

HANOI, VIETNAM, I ALMOST REMEMBER!
I remember Ho Chi Min's tiny home on the enormous palace grounds where the Communist-Democratic leader shunned living in the large grey state house he was offered. He was a, "man of the people," and very much revered. We waited in a long line at his huge, block-long, gray, stone tomb where he laid in state.

My husband gloried in seeing the lakes, the stone monuments, the folk-art and temples of the beautiful city again on our Indochina Zoom tour through the Asian Art Museum during Covid. The purple Jacaronda trees were all blooming and beginning to carpet the ground and the sky was so blue.

I was throwing up all over the carpeted halls, the bathroom and the beautiful bedroom of our hotel for the rest of our tour of Hanoi in 2001. A gorgeous lady doctor fed me tea slowly as I lay in bed mourning my loss. It took a day and a half for me to recuperate but that terrible time took two city tours away.

The next day, before my husband left without me for his trip to Halong Bay, he tried to pay the hotel for the doctor and the damage I had done. The hotel refused to accept.

My camera bag was embarrassing. Filthy, torn everywhere, and streaked with black, it had seen Europe, India and all the other places my heavy camera parts had been.

I plopped it in the wastebasket in the hotel. I felt I couldn't even give it away. When I returned to my room it was sitting on the top of the bureau. I tried to get rid of it in the basket the same way the next day, but it happened, again. I couldn't leave it there. I finally took it away with me.

Even the water puppets couldn't make up for the time I lost. I think of Hanoi kindly because of the lovely people. How could they have endured such terrible wars, survived, forgiven, and rebuilt such a beautiful city?

India

Krishna and Radha on top of the mountain c Helen Ann Licht

India

How do you capture the magic

Of a red desert sun on a hill,

Camels and men all around us

Turbans yellow and pink, sitting still?

HELEN ANN LICHT

The full moon has risen behind us,

With Venus and Mars up above.

Oh, which is the ultimate moment

Of an Indian trip that I love?

Was it festival dawn on the Ganges,

Fireworks in a palace so white,

The elephants and the pink city,

Oh, which do I think of tonight?

The temples in old Khadurajo

That the Chandelas built long ago,

The Taj and the Red Fort at Agra,

Shah Jahan in his prison, Oh no!

From the walls of the old Fort Golconda,

To the bangles and bracelets we wore,

Tanjore paintings and life in the city,

Or the Pichvai at old Deogarh,

The boat on the lake at Udaipur,

Or the caves at the edge of Bombay,

No, the best of the trip was a country

That we know we'll return to someday.

Bombay, 1997

My India

"**I** 'LL BUY YOU THIS BOOK on India if you'll never ask me to take you there." This was the statement made by my new husband, Norman, as I looked at the large picture book in a beautiful bookstore in 1958. It was not a hard promise to make. I had never even thought of going there.

Times change. In 1976 I was a 39 –year-old painter of brightly colored primitive visions. My three children were in their teens, and I was tired of volunteering. I wrote myself a strong recommendation and handed it to my painting teacher, Lundy, to sign. I was accepted into the University of California on the basis of my paintings.

I was almost ready for my second B.A. in studio art at Cal, when I walked by an open door to a class with a screen full of brilliant Indian miniatures, the colorful paintings from ancient manuscripts and books. *That's for me!* I said to myself, and enrolled for a third B.A., in art history. I went on to take the docent course at the Asian Art Museum in San Francisco.

I loved the carved temples, the folk art, and the charming people. My husband was always interested in the Far East because of the jewels. Norman became interested in India after we visited Borobudur Temple and Prambanam Temple in Indonesia.

He refused our friends who first asked us to go to India with them. One year later, we were in the backseat of a car when he said, "I think I'll go to India." Our friends in the front seat said, "We'll go too." We went straight to the travel agent, who happened to be our dinner hostess. She booked us on an art treasures tour of Northern India and Nepal with

Swans, a British company. We took two tours with Swans, one in the north and one in the south. Our friends who invited us initially were on our second tour.

After that we went twice with Margy Boyd, an exciting and charismatic leader. We tried to take a fifth tour to Bhubeneshwar, Puri, and the temple of Konarak in Northeast India with Margy's Indian travel agent, Sanjay Aurora, but age caught up with us, and we could only dream about it.

Bombay (Mumbai), 1986

WE FELL INTO A NOISY jumble of people of all sizes, colors, and dress, talking in many different languages, gesturing wildly and crowding us on all sides. The arrival room was hot. The walls were bare. The people there were so different and amazing. One woman was dressed in patterned, brown Balinese batik pant, scarf, and trim. Another wore an embroidered navy-blue outer garment over deep pink jamas along with a scarf, gold nose ring, tika, and diamonds. They were elbowed by a heavy woman in a black and red monkey patterned dress. Sheep herders wore dirty brown skins and sandals. Men dressed in white robes with Arab headdresses and Sikhs in bright red and yellow turbans mingled around the small, square room.

We found ourselves standing next to a young Muslim butcher, who killed goats and had their skins tanned in Madras to make purses and wallets to sell in Singapore. A yoga teacher from Ottawa who was living in Saudi Arabia and another from Pasadena had visited India four times. Indian people are very expressive and wildly gregarious. Everyone was shouting and jumping around. It was an international throng at the arrival line in the Mumbai Airport, late at night.

After a line for our passports, we got in another line for customs. Most people were bodily searched. Open, honey-colored suitcases were piled high with colorful cotton clothes that had been roughly rummaged through by customs. Their contents had to be forced back into the cases, which were then tied together with a wide rope. One man had to open all his packages from Hong Kong, including every drawer in a beautiful Chinese lacquer chest. Rolls of bedding lay open on the ground. Kitchen appliances were exposed in their boxes.

Our friend, Frances, found a man who let us through the door without inspection. Nobody hurried. It was after 11:00 p.m. There was one small car waiting for us when we finally were able to leave the airport and emerge in the dark outside. We were four large people with eight pieces of luggage. We couldn't fit in. Thomas, our greeter, had to make the long drive into town to look for another car for our luggage, and we had to wait.

When the second car finally arrived, we rode on a road with no lights. People were supposed to drive on the left side. The roads were marked into lanes with sandy shoulders, but nobody paid attention to that. Cars drove all over the road, diving in between other cars, bikes, and motorcycles.

Some of the streets were divided, but some had cars swerving straight toward us, barely missing. Drivers didn't put on their headlights—Thomas, our driver, said, "It was not to bother the oncoming cars." When a car came straight toward us, the lights came on. It was 11:30 at night, and our driver sped along. We had just passed the peak traffic. When he would come to a bunch of cars, about four abreast, he'd slam on the brakes and screech to a stop. At other times he'd race between and in front of cars in the middle of the white lines.

All of the cars were old. The khaki taxis were owned by the drivers, the black ones were owned by the taxi company. At around midnight, many people were walking by the sides of the road in groups of one, two or three.

Eventually we came to the shanties, with dark holes for entrances and what looked like rotting pieces of wood on the walls. They were lined up on either side of the road with no space in between. Behind them were peeling, old, white, taller buildings. It was hard to see the people cooking in front because of the dim light and the smoke. We passed open air places to eat, author Salmon Rushdi's "green cafes," garish movie houses, and a giant overpass with many, many people sleeping beneath it.

Because Thomas took a shortcut, we didn't pass Marine Drive. All of a sudden, we came upon a huge, lit-up open building with people sleeping inside and others walking all around it. Thomas said it was Victoria Station. We passed it so fast it was hard to see the gingerbread architecture and turrets. Next, we recognized Flora Fountain in the middle of a maidan (square). It was a small Victorian fountain with no water. Thomas told us they turned it on only during the day.

After a long drive, we were at the Gateway to India and the jammed parking lot of the Taj Mahal Hotel. The cool, crowded lobby smelled musty. There were no rooms! About ten people from our plane were arguing at the marble desk:

"It's past midnight, we're tired, we just flew in from Singapore."

"I'm sorry, we're oversold ..."

"People haven't left, and it's too bad."

Nothing happened. We stood around. Finally, they told us to go to the coffee shop to eat. We met two jewelers from Vancouver who had just received a room. They complained it was inadequate.

Frances and Richard received their room first, in the old section. Around 1:00 a.m. we received a room in the new section. It was not made up. It smelled of cigarettes. We waited. After it was made up, we slept fitfully. The room was high in the plain new section. Everything was dark outside. When we awoke, we looked out the window at tall, close, cement slums with cotton clothes and blankets hanging from open windows. Sleeveless, smoking men in undershirts were standing on balconies. We gobbled down two dosas (pancakes with potato filling) in the restaurant for breakfast.

The waves lapped against the large white stones in front of the Gateway to India, the huge colonial marble arch across the street from the hotel. The arch was built by the British, who also built the roads. It didn't look to me like anything much had progressed since they left in 1950. The sun turned the water deep blue. White-shirted young men were standing and lying about. A bent, wrinkled, old lady was quietly sweeping the road with a meagre handmade broom.

Stepping across beggars lying on the chipped sidewalk, we walked two blocks behind our hotel to the Prince of Wales Museum. Chipped Ellora stone sculptures were in the overgrown Victorian garden and on the entry floor. Large red sandstone pillars surrounded the three-storied courtyard. It was capped by a glass dome. Many blue-and white-uniformed children were visiting the museum.

On the first floor we found a wonderland of miniatures surrounding the courtyard. They were hard to see with the magnifying glasses provided, because the light reflected on the glass frames. The famous Moghul paintings of Durbars (audiences of Shah Jahan) were there in all their bright one-dimensional splendor. There were also beautiful Indian line drawings and contemporary portraits.

Frances found a small hidden door, and we walked in. Inside a small room with a glass case, we bought beautiful portfolios of museum reproductions of the paintings for two rupees each. The men unlocked a safe and showed us more portfolios. We bought those too.

In the afternoon we embarked from the arch for the island of Elephanta. Many small boats were bobbing in the harbor. Our launch was pushed off by a small boy with a bamboo pole. We passed an island with an atomic plant. We were told it was "built by Pakistan and Russia for peaceful use." We passed another small island with a military museum.

When we arrived at Elephanta Island we took a smaller barge to the sandy shore. The entrance reminded me of Yelapa in Mexico. It was very primitive. Trees were growing out of the water. We climbed many wobbly, wooden stairs past cheap souvenir stands. Toothless women posed in cheesy costumes with two layers of brass pots on their heads. Two rupees bought a picture, monkeys included.

At the top of the stairs a landslide had buried the original entrance. We walked around. The huge Hindu and Buddhist sculpture of the declining style of the seventh century were impossible to photograph because of the darkness in the open caves. I couldn't capture the magnificent statue of the three-headed Shiva. It was too enormous for my heavy old camera and 1000mm film.

TRAVELS WITH AN ARTIST

We photographed huge columns surmounted by cushion capitals that surrounded the cosmic dance of Shiva. Baby Ganesh with his elephant head was stamping out evil. Shiva, The Destroyer, was there too. The beautiful Indian woman who led us around the magnificent sculpture was the editor of a national travel magazine.

Norman's birthday dinner on January 16th was at the Tandoori Restaurant in the Taj Hotel. He was able to share his cake with a San Francisco friend we ran into who was traveling on another tour. The old section of the hotel is beautiful, with lovely wood around the courtyard, lovely material in the shop, and a lovely gallery, but we had no time to shop. That was left for another year.

On other tours, we ran into our friend Mary Ann Lutzker, my teacher's assistant at Cal. Once we met her at the observatory in Jaipur. She visited us for cocktails with her mother in Jaipur. We met for tea in the tea room of the Taj Mahal Hotel on another trip.

1986

Rajiv Ghandhi

THE BRIDE'S AUNT WAS WORKING over a selection of copperware bowls to use in the wedding ritual. At the bottom left of the stairs was a small section with thin poles and a cover on top that looked like a chuppah. She invited us down to see it and tell us about it before the wedding. The party was about to start.

The hotel lobby had a moon-shaped stairway leading down to the party rooms below. It was 1981, the evening of our farewell dinner on our first trip to India. We were staying at the Taj Mahal Hotel with Swans, a London-based company that featured tours of exotic Eastern art and architecture.

We stood halfway down the stairway, watching the guests arrive. Tall, handsome men in black tuxedos and colorful turbans with diamond stickpins attached and beautiful women in red, pink, green, blue, and gold embroidered saris came in. They wore diamonds around their wrists, necks, and ears, and even in their noses. It was a bejeweled rainbow. There was a red carpet. It was rumored that there would be an important guest. The identity of the guest was unknown.

We watched the terrified teenage bride being pushed down the stairs by relatives. She looked very frightened and tense, as she was about to meet her future husband for the first time. She was dressed in a bright pink and green skirt sewn with filigree silver jewels, bare waist, and short, tight green blouse. She was very attractive, wearing a large, round nose ring and a puja in the middle of her forehead. Her straight, black hair was drawn back in a bun, and she wore a veil on her head. She seemed overwhelmed and unhappy.

My friend's husband pushed something aside on the floor. It looked like a silver chewing-gum wrapper. He picked it up, and it tumbled open into a filigree droplet in his hands. It was a light silver jewel from her gown.

Soon our two husbands became anxious.

"Hurry up, or we'll be late for the farewell dinner."

"We'll just wait here."

"Don't be late."

My friend Frances, another woman, her daughter, and I didn't leave. The men rushed upstairs to the dinner. We stood on the stairs and waited.

The outside doors opposite to us opened, and in walked Rajiv Gandhi and his beautiful wife, Sonia. He was dressed in a plain gray Nehru suit and hat, she in a shiny green sari. Her hair was swept back under her veil, and she was as beautiful as a movie star. She looked like Grace Kelly. Handsome, young, Prime Minister Gandhi smiled at us and folded his hands in a gesture of namaste. We were late for the farewell dinner. We sat at the end of the table, dazed.

Six months later, a sari-clad young woman elbowed her way to the front of the outdoor political rally where Gandhi was speaking. She detonated a bomb on her body and blew up both of them.

Hyderabad

"**Y**OU'RE FROM CALIFORNIA—I JUST LOVE San Jose," said the glamorous movie star in the ruined palace of the old Fort Golconda, while posing for photos with our group of San Franciscans among the kleig lights and trappings of India's immense movie industry. Under the nickname "Bollywood," it serves potboilers to the largest movie-going public in the world, producing everything from sugary romantic musicals to wild adventure. Many Indian politicians got their start as movie producers or stars.

The huge artificial set consisted of two tiers of arches on the ancient walls, hung with scarves and saris in reds, greens, and purples. A curving clothesline held laundry, and banners floated all around. Huge antiquated jars rested at the side of a rusty old moss-covered well. The cast and musicians were dressed in cheap, bright saris and colorful turbans. Sitars and other musical instruments were lying all over the ground. The added color enhanced our excitement from being on the huge stone fortress on the hill.

We were exploring the famous crenelated ruins five miles outside of Hyderabad, a Muslim city in central India. Located high on the Deccan Plain in the province of Andhra Pradesh, it was an impressive site.

Laughing, uniformed schoolgirls in white sailor tops and black skirts kept talking to us and giggling among themselves as we climbed the long, stone slab stairs. They showed us their hennaed hands and offered to take our pictures, as they thought we looked quite strange and exotic.

After climbing partway, we entered the fort through a double gate large enough for two or three elephants to pass. It was one of four open gates of the original eight. Guards with crescent sabers, dressed in black boots, white balloon pants, red vests, billowing white shirts, and red hats guarded the entrance. The imposing, wooden doors were ajar. They were studded with golden spikes. The door jams were carved out of stone with tales from Indian folklore (Jataka tales).

From the gate, you could see more walls encircling the heights. It might have been the gate that Aurangzeb, the wicked Mughal leader, entered as he conquered old Golconda and brought the Kol-noor diamond back to the Red Fort in Delhi for his father, Shah Jahan. At the time of the Silk Road, the ancient caravan route, Hyderabad was famous for diamonds. The industry has dwindled. Now pearls and silk are its well-known products.

Ruins of other old palaces, stables, and mosques came into sight around every corner of our climb. Each angle was perfect for a photograph. The only problem was elimination.

We looked down at a distant view of the tombs of the early rulers of Hyderabad, the Qutb Shahi. These Turkoman people were the builders of the fort. Many of the bulbous-ceilinged monuments on the plain below had remnants of original tiles and decorative stuccowork. The black basalt graves inside had simple inscriptions.

The Salar Jung Museum in Hyderabad held inlaid, translucent jade bowls, statuary, weapons, and Indian paintings. The miniatures ranged from early Jain palm-leaf prayer books, kalpasutras, to colorful seventeenth-century Mughal manuscripts. Most of the works were originally found in books. They represented all the different Indian states and time periods. Hunting, dancing (Ragamalas), love stories, and Mughal portraits were painted in the stylized manner of each state.

The most important monument in the center of town is the sixteenth-century Char Minar. It is considered the masterpiece of Qutb Shahi architecture. It was impossible to enter because of auto traffic all around it. It is now covered with graffiti. The building was designed as a perfect square, with four arches for passage. Above the lower arches were rows of smaller arches and a stringcourse anchored by four domed minarets. We were told about the central dome but were not able to see it. The building is so large, it was visible from all sides and from a great distance. Shops in India are usually small and built by hand.

The commerce around the Char Minar was part of the fun. Merchants hawked from carts full of starfruit, custard fruit, silver coated candy, chalk, buttons, and tikas (the marks on the women's foreheads). On the crowded side streets were shops selling bangles arranged floor to ceiling, wedding dresses, saris, silver, crinkle silks, masks, bidri ware (inlaid metalwork), other handicrafts, and Hyderabad's famous pearls.

We couldn't get over the fact that so many young, beautiful women in saris were covered with diamonds. They wore diamond necklaces, rings, and earrings on airplanes, trains, in the streets, and around poverty and barefoot beggars every day. The diamonds were small but plentiful. Even at weddings tall, handsome men in tuxedos wear rainbow-colored turbans decorated with large, diamond stick pins. At most upper-caste Indian weddings, all the men and women wear a plethora of diamonds. Even the elephants at the weddings wear diamonds.

Hyderabad is famous for trading. It is a tradition that has lasted from the time of the Silk Road in the fifteenth century. Visiting Hyderabad was like being in a giant carnival, and I, like the silk traders of old, shopped and shopped.

Deogarh (c) Helen Ann Licht

Deogarh

"**E**XCUSE ME," I SHRIEKED, AS my bare elbow jabbed the soft, silky surface of the sacred white cow as it ambled languidly down the sandy street in Deogarh. Chattering young women in red, green, and gold saris were skipping beside us, their silver anklets jingling joyfully as they passed. Wrinkled old men in white cotton suits and gray Nehru hats walked beside us, dangling wooden prayer beads from black books they carried.

Barefoot, brown-skinned boys in white, unbuttoned shirts and black shorts played kick the can while weaving around the swirling people and animals. A ragged, long-haired peddler held a swaying, round thin pole on which mysteriously balanced on high a flat platform of sugarcoated buns and breads.

It was noon. The teeming street was hot. The scorching sun soaked our thin-sleeved arms with sweat. Our light linen shirts and straw hats hung limply. We felt like we were in

Rundown, dusty white buildings cascaded with bougainvillea lined the east side of the road. The open windows looked black, leading to the invisible insides. Trampled plants grew like weeds on the left side of the road due to the constant torrent of human life.

On the west side were handmade wooden tables full of food. Yellow bananas, lemony starfruit and buddha's hands, purple mangosteen and aubergine, orange carrots, persimmons, and various other raw vegetables were sold next to powdery pyramids of makeup in garish colors of red, blue, magenta, and black. Streetside stands loaded with glowing bangles and henna stood next to counters stacked with silk saris in colors from gold and silver to a virtual rainbow. Painted pottery statues of Hindu gods Shiva, Ganesha, and Kali stood among batiked banners, quilts, and hand painted shrines

The succulent smell of roast pig from the temporary barbecues set up along the teeming street melded with the smells of turmeric, cardamom, cinnamon, and other fragrant spices tantalizing us as we passed. The smoke mixed with the pungent smell of cow dung.

Dirty, ragged children followed us, begging for a coin. Thin old men were washing their teeth with twigs and spitting in the long, thin sewers that lined either side of the road.

Suddenly, a wobbly wooden cart barreled through the middle of the street scattering people and animals to both sides. The grizzled, toothless driver of the emaciated horse seemed not to notice the tumult he created or the noisy rattling of the iron pots, pans, and other metal junk piled up inside his open plank-sided top. The show was in the streets.

A small, seductive, stone Hindu temple was at the end of the sandy road. The sweet smell of incense burning from the lighted votive candles filled the air. Bald, saffron-robed pilgrims poured from the entrance gate. The single tower loomed above as we approached. Several men with shaved heads were circumambulating below outside the temple on the raised plinths, paying homage to the three-dimensional carvings of the celebrated Hindu epic, the Ramayana, on the outside walls. These were the tales of the early life of the gods Rama and Sita. They were considered the books of the unlettered. The pilgrims moved slowly from left to right. They then paid homage to the stark, black lingam in the dark inner chamber, the garbhagriha.

We strolled back to our charming hotel to marvel at the red, blue, and green stained glass windows in the stone ogival arches above the small window seats that filled the alcoves. We bought shimmering silk scarfs and stoles from a grateful local merchant in his tiny shop along the way. This was the India I loved.

The Elephants

"I 'LL TAKE IT!" SHOUTED MARGY, our leader, from her shaky perch on top of the enormous elephant she was riding. The peddler on the other side of the wide canyon was waving an embroidered, white bedspread. We were halfway up the high mountain on the way to Amber Palace in Rajistan. She knew how to shop, and all of India was her bazaar.

The elephants lumbered slowly up the hill, veering to the left as we rolled to the right and to the right as we rolled to the left. We were sitting high atop a wobbly, double, wooden saddle, decorated with brightly patterned painting, cross stitches, and jangling bells. The bumpy ride in the line of pachyderms reached all the way to Amber Fort, a sixteenth-century royal Moghul complex. It was built of yellow and pink sandstone and white marble, with luxuriously decorated mosaic, mirrored, painted, and tiled rooms, domes, and pools. The hilltop palace is an imposing UNESCO tourist site, towering above the Aravalli hills of India. We looked way back to the walled, square, Moghul garden and lake below. We could see the town of Jaipur through the mist, six miles away.

Prehensile miniature monkeys scrambled all over our path, hanging from trees, screaming, and guarding their babies along the way. Their noisy chirps accompanied the banging clip clop of the large animals we were riding. Peacocks screeched and unfolded their turquoise feathers. Flocks of small birds arced above. The smell of elephant dung was coupled with the fragrance of flowers and cinnamon. It was an airy, energizing, exciting, and uncomfortable journey.

The deep ravine beside our path was covered with treetops resembling matted gray hair, about half a mile below. Across the ravine, on the faraway, downward path, waved a vigorous, dense, line of white-clothed peddlers wearing pink, green, and yellow turbans. They were waving small wooden shrines, scarves, t-shirts, rugs, and jewelry to our laughing, upward-bound caravan.

One man on the other side of the ravine held out a pale, white bedspread full of colorful designs. You have to think fast. Margy bargained with the man on the descent and found she had bought a stunning and very unusual white, hand-embroidered bedspread—to glow in her bedroom for the rest of her life.

She taught me how to shop!

Varanasi

"THE BHARAT KALA BHAVAN IN Varanasi—you must see it!" My friend, Mary Anne, who teaches Indian art at Mills, insisted. "It's the most famous miniature painting museum in India, and it's connected to old Benares University." I told Margy, our tour leader, and she was enthusiastic. "Of course, I want to go, too. We'll definitely see it together."

We arrived in Varanasi, the former Benares, for the second time. I was excited and a little bit scared about exploring this dense, mysterious city in more depth. We were met by the same rigid, old guide that we had had on our last trip. "We'll go to the Ganges to view the ghats, see ancient temples and mosques, and after lunch we'll go to Sarnath, where Buddha preached his first sermon." It was the identical tour we had had the first time we were there, absolutely nothing more. He didn't even ask if this was our second or third visit.

We had only one night and one full day in the holy city. I was downcast. I knew I would never be able to return. "Don't make a fuss!" said my husband. I left for our room to mope before dinner. I was missing what I had looked forward to ever since the trip was first planned. Right away the phone rang. Margy had hired a taxi to take my husband and me to the Bhavan, the art museum of Benares University, the next afternoon.

My husband felt torn. "I think I should go with the tour to Sarnath. It's the right thing to do, even though we've been there before." Margy, too, had to go with the tour, as she was the leader. I, alone, didn't want to miss the chance to explore the exotic, mysterious Bhavan.

At 4:00 a.m. the next day, before the heaviest heat, we were bused to the ghats, the immense, white, slab staircases leading down to the Ganges River. We walked to them through a small passage, past weathered old mosques, temples, and palaces. The smell of dust, musk, and cow dung greeted us as we strolled along. Near the bottom of the broad stone steps stood hundreds of women in rainbow-colored saris, black kol-lined eyes, forehead bindis, and raised, clasped hands, with clothed bodies half submerged in the Ganges, giving thanks to Shiva for the blessing of their husbands. **My old camera was out of film!**

Barefoot men took their daily ablutions, washing, brushing their teeth, shaving, and relieving themselves in the water. A multitude of emaciated, grizzled, bald men with skimpy white dhotis wrapped around their waists swarmed the stairs, performing ceremonial puja, their quotidian acts of worship. Men in white cotton suits and Nehru hats were hanging around in groups.

The sound of bells was everywhere. Crossed-legged, bare-chested flute and sitar players added to the cacophony. The swaying crowd grew to monstrous proportions. There was a complete absence of open space. Luminous haze covered the huge blue-gray moon as it slowly sank into the waters below, making a quiet, surreal scene where they met.

After we descended the stairs and entered our open floating skiff to embark, it was surrounded by other long, flat boats, with hawkers peddling iridescent silk scarves, cheap jewelry, ivory, woven carpets, and shrines. Boatmen held up long, green paper boxes full of miniature carved and painted wooden figures, deities such as Shivas, Krishnas, Durgas, Hanumans, and Ganeshas, as well as cute Indian military men in red, white, yellow, and blue uniforms holding bugles and beating drums. From our boat we saw the sinking Hindu temple, steaming with smoke from the cremated bodies on the pyres outside. Mourners were milling around, having made pilgrimages from all over India to scatter their beloved's ashes in the Ganges.

We left the ghats when it became light and pushed our way through pulsing streets, passing honking cyclists, beggars, and pyramids of oranges. The smell of incense, curry, cinnamon, cardamom, and barbecued pigs followed us as we strolled.

After lunch, I went alone to the Bhavan. I rode in the back seat of the taxi with the windows down in order to inhale the scents of the road. We followed red-clay streets past slim palm trees and tiny, unevenly spaced white houses to the university. A young friend of the driver rode along with him in the front seat.

When we arrived, the three of us entered a small, square room. A glass showcase about four and a half feet high, containing folders of souvenir museum reproductions of the paintings inside, took up most of the space. Five or six young men in open-neck, short-sleeved white shirts were listlessly lounging on the top and sides of the case. Other young men were languishing against the walls, doing nothing. They admonished us:

You can't go in!

Why?

There are no lights!

I came from San Francisco just to see it!

There are no lights!

I'm with the San Francisco Museum of Modern Art!"

(a little lie, I was only on a tour)

You can't go in!

I came from so far!

There are no lights!

I'll never get back.

OK! We'll turn the lights on for fifteen minutes.

Great!

Leave your backpack, your money, and all your stuff with us on top of the glass case. I did!

One of the men found a key and opened the door. The driver, the young boy, and I ran in. Inside were four enormous white rooms, hung with hundreds of hand-painted Indian miniatures. Most were taken from old books. Each was framed and painted in the distinctive style of each of the separate provinces of India: early Jain palm-leaf manuscripts; colorful, stylized paintings from Bikanar; hunting scenes from Bihar, Mandu, and Gugarat; and flat, sixteenth-century realistic Mughal court paintings that showed the durbar of Shah Jahan. We were overwhelmed. We started to make our way along the walls.

Fifteen minutes!

We had barely begun when the lights went off. Black, Black, Black, everything was black! There was a complete blackout!

"Don't worry," the driver's young friend gleefully said. He ran outside to the taxi and produced a flashlight. We saw the entire four huge rooms by light of the flash.

Dazzled, we left the Bhavan around 4:00 p.m. I collected my backpack and wallet and asked the young men sitting on the showcase if I could buy the folder of reproductions as a memory to take home. They vehemently said, "Too late, it's after four. We locked it up!"

On the way back to the hotel, the taxi driver stopped his car by a small, pastel-painted Hindu temple. Two young men showed me around. Together we smelled the incense and saw the beautiful, wooden building by candlelight. That afternoon was the best part of the trip for me.

I was still in a trance when I told my husband about our exciting experience. He said the tour to Sarnath was a repeat of where we had been before. One of the old beggars had even given him back his alms—she said it was "too little." He was very sad he had missed the Bhavan.

Varanasi (c) Helen Ann Licht

Margy

I remember when the bus stopped in the New Mexico desert. The passengers jumped

picked out the one unusual beautiful set of prayer beads. By the time the ladies went through the shop, it was gone. She was an experienced shopper.

Red haired, exotic, charismatic Margy was a great teacher She found out of the way places and covered the world. With her, we crossed deserts, slept in tents, and visited caves. We met all kinds of artists and a world I never could have seen by myself.

She was always individually dressed, with bright flowing tunics and skirts topped with large, artist-designed, unusual, original jewelry. Her husband, Nick, was a yachtsman who accompanied her on a few of her special trips. She was from an old-line, Episcopalian family, in San Francisco. Their son converted to Muslim. Her daughter was Jewish, married to a rabbi. A very interesting, unconventional family. Her home was like a private art gallery on a hill in Pacific Heights. She knew everybody.

She once sat me for dinner on the left of a long robed, heavy-set, gay collector in his antique filled home in the Majorelle Gardens in Marrakesh, Morocco. With her, I visited the caves of Dun Huang and rode a camel in the China desert, had dinner in 17th Century palaces in India, met all kinds of artists and visited Joan Miro's studio in Majorca.

I missed a big party in Vienna. (Margy knew people). The next day, Monday, the Vienna museums were all closed. They opened them for her. She divided her tour in two parts and we were assigned to the Vienna Art Museum with Henry Hopkins, the former director of the San Francisco Museum of Modern Art. It was such a treat discussing the 1543 Cellini salt cellar, the Breugel and Bosc paintings, alone, with him in the uncrowded Viennese palace. Museum directors and insiders would always accompany her tours. With Margy's wisdom, charisma and energy she was a Pied Piper to her followers.

Three large buses went to the Grapevine to see the yellow umbrellas of Cristo. So many San Francisco socialites were traveling with her. Doris Fisher from the Gap was loading up on cheap umbrella T-shirts at one of the makeshift stands. Among the hundreds of important people who were at that country bus stop, Margy suddenly ran across me. She made me feel like I had made her day, because among the many San Francisco people on her tour, I was there.

Margy was let out of the Museum of Modern Art in San Francisco by a new young director because of ageism. It was a terrible blow to everyone who loved her, but she took it well, She arranged to take her large following on private tours. She never mentioned how frightened and upset she was. She still had connections. "I can go it alone" she told us. She hired an assistant and continued to lead us all over the world.

Many years later she tired. She broke her foot in the shower in India. She survived her sister's accidental death while she was in Normandy. She had to stay in the hotel two days to rest and recuperate, but she led the tour until the end. "I will still go on" she said, until she couldn't. Could a woman like her go on forever?

No one is immortal. She was in her seventies or eighties when she finally had to quit. Nobody could reach her. We all called, sent cards, invitations and flowers, to no avail.

She enriched the lives of so many people and then she was gone.

The White House

My Mistake

I MADE A BIG MISTAKE—OR DID I?! It was the 1990s. President George Bush Sr. was in the White House. It was the time of the Viet Nam war. I had protested the war! I had marched with Women for Peace and written many letters to both of my Congressmen and to the newspapers. I was a Democrat with liberal values. My husband was in business but very supportive of me. He only said, "Do not march by the family store." One of my letters was printed in the *Chronicle*. Norman told me, "A customer came in gave me hell." Good for Norman!

California politics were exciting to me. Barbara Boxer and Dianne Feinstein were two Jewish woman Senate candidates. I hosted coffees for both of them in my home with my politically involved friends. We charged twenty-five dollars per person for the campaign, and I was so happy to help. I knew them, or at least I thought I did.

I went to camp and to college with Dianne Feinstein. She used to write to me in Weiser. (I should have saved her letters.) Diane was one of the smartest young women I knew. She was a graduate of the Coro Program, a prestigious political study group of recent college graduates, an advocate for prison reform, and the former mayor of San Francisco.

Barbara Boxer's campaign manager was the husband of another summer camp friend, an artist like me. Barbara Boxer and her manager even stopped by our home for a twenty-five dollars per person party—on their way that evening to Blackhawk Country Club in Danville for a twenty-five thousand dollar per person party. She was so charming and personal, and she took time to admire my paintings. She stood on the small rise in front of our fireplace mantel and said to the guests, "I am some tough New York Jew." I loved her and always followed her on the television and in the newspapers.

In the midst of campaigning for those two outstanding women, an invitation came from the White House. My husband and I were invited to dinner. *President and Mrs. Bush will be in attendance* was printed on the invitation. It was large, cream-colored, and engraved in gold. Red, white, and blue ribbons floated from the four sides. It was one of the most beautiful invitations I have ever seen. I didn't know why I had received the invitation. I asked my husband if he had ever contributed to the Republican Party, and he swore he hadn't. Two days later, another invitation arrived. It was for cocktails at a famous hotel, the Hay-Adams, given by the conservative senator from Contra Costa County, where we lived. I didn't vote for him. *What should I do?*

Paul Newman and various movie stars were protesting the Viet Nam war and refusing the Kennedy honors. *Why shouldn't I?* Young boys were dying in a war few people wanted. I was for abortion rights and against the death penalty, the Patriot Act, the invasion of Panama, the Viet Nam war and the Iraq war.

I now realize the invitation probably was sent because my beautiful, blue painting of Mexico, *On the Zocalo, Oaxaca*, was hanging in the American Embassy in Lima, Peru, through the State Department Art in Embassies Program, courtesy of my San Francisco gallery, Interart. I didn't think about that at the time.

I didn't answer the invitation. I threw it away too fast. I now feel that that spontaneous act hurt my painting career. My husband would have gladly taken me to Washington for dinner in a beautiful room with the President. I didn't realize we received the invitation because of my donated painting. I wanted to be a famous artist and didn't know the invitation was about the embassy painting.

I lost my gallery and their support, even though it closed. I was so heady with the Democratic campaign that I couldn't understand that I could still support the party candidates and attend the dinner. I didn't answer the invitation on principle! I didn't want it in the local papers that I supported that president. For years, I was too embarrassed to mention it to anybody. I made a fast ethical decision. It was probably wrong.

The next Contra Costa senator was a democrat, Ellen Tauscher. I had very little contact with her or Dianne Feinstein or Barbara Boxer, when I showed my paintings at the B'nai B'rith Klutznick Museum in Washington, D.C., every year for the next three years.

When I was in Washington, I went through the White House dining room on a paid commercial tour. It seemed gold and white and like a fairytale. We could have had a beautiful evening to remember all our lives. I felt heavy remorse. I'll never be invited to dinner there again. Still, somehow, I still feel ethics are important.

Should I have gone and smiled and promoted my art by adding a White House dinner to my resume? I now look upon the late President Bush and his wife, Barbara, as a nice old couple. I could have shaken their hands.

I made a miserable mistake! Or did I?

Diamonds

I NEVER THOUGHT I'D BE A jeweler's wife. My grandparents had a small jewelry store in Seattle in the 1920s. It was gone by the time I was born. In my blissful youth, I would buy jewelry for under two dollars: a string of shells from a stand on the sand, painted plastic earrings from a street seller, or string-it-yourself colored-glass beads. I loved the bohemian look and the art jewelry from the museums. When you're young, everything you wear looks great.

In those years I received a proposal and a big diamond from a handsome young man. He had taken it out of his family's safe—a big ring for a young girl with very little jewelry experience or interest. The engagement didn't work out, and I gave him back the ring.

Diamonds just came to me. They were on the ring Norman slid on my finger as he kissed me under the chuppah—I still wear. My next diamond was a magnificent marquise, a romantic surprise from my husband. It came wrapped in a tuxedo box for no special occasion. I asked him to have it set in a simple, striated gold band. Norman thought the band was too plain when I wore it. He eventually talked me into a fancier band. My best friend saw my simple band and ordered one like it for her diamond. I missed my old band so much that I had one of my aunt's round diamonds set in it. It showed my taste wasn't so bad.

Norman invited me to a jewelry show in the Oakland store. A beautiful model passed by with a stylish sapphire-and-diamond ring on her slender finger. I admired it, and Norman gave it to me. It didn't look the same on my fingers as it did on her beautiful hands. My hands are arthritic now, even more than they were then. To have a husband like mine, who always thought of me, made me feel very special.

He gave me a very big diamond when he retired. He had been saving it for me. I had the diamond set in a gold band, not the platinum band with triangular side-diamonds he wanted for me. I worried it was too pretentious. I now regret it. I remember reading in a newspaper that actress Joan Collins received a brilliant five-carat diamond ring the same day I did. I hardly knew who she was, but her diamond made the newspapers.

I wore my big diamond whenever I had a bar mitzvah or a wedding with three or four parties on one weekend. Otherwise, it sat in the safe, where I never saw it. Some people gushed over it. My close friends really didn't care. What was so important to me was that Norman gave it to me. I loved the jeweler.

We journeyed to Asia to buy diamonds. From beautiful hotels I went sightseeing while he worked. When Norman retired, we stayed in dorms. We took classes in London, France, and Rome. I told people, "I graduated my husband from the Mauna Kea to the dorm." Sometimes in college dorms we even shared a bathroom. He was such a good sport.

We would window shop the fine jewelry stores wherever we were. We often ran into people who wore diamonds, which seemed such a hindrance. A Canadian woman from a class in Venice made me feel like I was in poverty when she saw my simple gold band. A woman at the table in a restaurant in the Ghetto said to me, "You must have beautiful diamonds." I replied, "I do, but I am here, and they are there." My clothes were old and wash-and-wear, and all Rome sparkled before me.

In India, so many young women in saris were covered with diamonds. They wore diamond necklaces, rings, and earrings on airplanes, trains, around poverty and barefoot beggars, every day. The diamonds were small but plentiful. We even watched a wedding where the tall, handsome men in tuxedos wore rainbow-colored turbans decorated with enormous diamond stickpins. Even the elephants wore diamonds. Of course, these were different from the single diamonds embedded in the noses and tummies of young and old people in America.

The sultry soprano sang the "Diamond Aria" in *The Tales of Hoffman* while flashing a huge multi-faceted, fake glass diamond. Strobe lights whirled around the ceiling and over the entire opera house. It was mesmerizing. Marilyn Monroe sang a charming song, "Diamonds are a Girl's Best Friend." Her whole body, especially her eyes, lit up when she sang. The song may be true for most people. Diamonds are security. They will last after someone loved is gone due to divorce, death, or other reasons. There's nothing like a diamond to flash and twinkle all over the psyche. I've seen how much it is desired, how much it means to so many people.

Our lives have changed. The diamonds are for the next generation to enjoy. As my mother once said, "It's only material." But the beautiful diamonds have never changed. They hold memories, security, and the knowledge that I was truly loved.

Lucky 2020

I FEEL LUCKY. THREE MONTHS AGO, I was in my bedroom with a feeling of *gratitude*. I was thinking about my life. I have accomplished most of my goals, and I am happy. My husband and I live in a beautiful home with a garden. Our family, our books and interests are all around us.

My eighty-seventh birthday was a wonderful week. We saw Joyce De Donato in Agrippina at the Metropolitan opera movie Saturday morning and enjoyed a delicious Chinese dinner with Asian Art Museum friends on our 64th anniversary, March 3. We had dinner at a lovely restaurant with my daughter, Lisa, and her partner on March 4. She brought me a beautiful bouquet of sunflowers. I saw an afternoon play at Berkeley Rep with my friends on Thursday, attended an Asian art history class at the museum Friday morning, and a fabulous ballet Friday night, only to top it off with Carol Strayed's play, *Tiny Beautiful Things*, on Saturday afternoon. Dinner was with our son, David, along with Sharon and Wyatt on Sunday night. My grandson, Brian, shares a birthday with me, but he is a doctor in New York, so we couldn't celebrate together.

Spending time in San Francisco and with my family was the best celebration in the world. The ballet Friday night was *Midsummer's Night's Dream*, a dream of a ballet with one hundred dancers on stage at a time, Yuan Yuan Tan, Tiits Helimet a full orchestra, and a chorus. The stage designers, the lighting designers, and probably another twenty-five or thirty people had worked on the exciting, demanding program for years. It was the premiere of one of the best ballets I have ever seen. It closed permanently when the curtain went down.

Then the entire city center stopped. The symphony canceled its programs, including Michael Tilson Thomas's final New York and European tour. Herbst Theater, the Veteran's Building and the City Hall went black. One by one the theaters canceled, the little and the big ones, as did the museums, art galleries, libraries, sports venues, and all classes. Restaurants were faced with cancellations and closures. Mom and pop stores closed, and people scrambled to try to patch up the suffering homeless. Churches, mosques, and synagogues closed. Cruise ships were anchored outside the ports, not letting sick and desperate passengers disembark.

All over the country, people were admonished to stay inside their homes, regardless of their ability to buy food and necessities. People hoarded. Toilet paper and sanitary hand wipes were in short supply. People were told to wear masks and then were told not to wear them.

The loss to the Bay Area and the world is overwhelming. The musicians, the dancers, the opera singers, the visual artists, as well as the producers, the stagehands, the restaurateurs, and the shops, will need years to recover stability and the money they will lose, if they recover at all. The composers expecting premieres of their new works, the museums about to open, Michael Tilson Thomas' last trip to New York and Europe with the symphony, the fundraisers, the summer programs, and the honorees planning debuts will all lose, and the Olympic athletes will have to train another year or give up their hopes.

Students will miss graduation ceremonies and proms, suffering school at home, and those studying abroad have had to cut short their programs and fly home. I feel so sorry for them, after all they have achieved. People now have to be cautious and wear masks in public. Hospitals were unprepared for the mysterious, contagious coronavirus (COVID-19) that leaped from China through Europe and Africa and landed in the United States.

Our country was in the middle of feisty election debates. The Democrats had outstanding contenders, but the fear persisted about who had the strength to beat a threatening incumbent. Rallies were canceled, and campaigning was stopped. Money was thrown about by those who had it and attacked by those who didn't. I felt so much money was lost that could have been used for schools, infrastructure, and medical care. Women were worried about their right to choose, the Supreme Court choices, and climate change. The poor immigrants were in limbo, with sick and separated families begging for attention in horrible situations.

I realize that these things may be nothing compared to getting the terrible virus. It is a difficult time, and I am trying to keep my sanity. It is hard, especially when all luncheons, book groups, and classes are canceled.

For me, it brings a good and much-needed rest, a time to telephone friends and catch up on my reading, even though I find it hard to concentrate. I am anxious for the people who are sick and worried who will be next.

We have a lovely San Francisco apartment with a view (last seen in early March). I hear the residents there are singing from their balconies every night at six o'clock. They receive a different song sheet every day from the manager. I feel it would be hard to live in a one-bedroom apartment confined to your space every day. I don't know where they get their food, as so many restaurants and coffee shops around there are closed. I understand food delivery is booming, but many people eat alone.

My single friends seem isolated. The elevators must be sanitized, and only one person or someone living with them is allowed in at a time. They must wear a mask even when they go to dump their garbage or wash their clothes. The pool and patio, the gym and the hot tub, are closed. The San Francisco sidewalks are not wide enough to allow people to distance themselves by six feet. I call my friends from time to time, but we are all so busy. They are not so lucky as I am.

We had planned a superb spring with operas, ballets, plays, symphonies, and an interesting Asian art class on the meaning and symbols of death in the Orient. We were looking forward to our granddaughter's Ph.D. graduation from Cal in June and her wedding one week later. We were healthy, hoping to enjoy them all.

Then coronavirus came along. The summer is over now, and we are enjoying a much-needed rest at home. Because of my meditative practice of gratitude, my happiness carried me through the cancellations, the hardships, the losses, the worries, and the terrible scare of losing my family, losing businesses I loved, the loss of the arts, the postponement of our two grand-daughters' weddings, and the terrible poverty of the people on the street. I am aware that life will never be the same as long as I live.

The enrichment offered through the television and the computer is amazing. We've watched operas, plays, and interviews and traveled the world vicariously. I hope other people are doing the same. I contacted some of my friends in Italy and China, and they have texted back that they are well.

Making three meals a day, keeping house, walking, and the computer are taking up the entire day. For us, it's merely poignant. Norman's tennis game will never be the same. The arts as we knew them will never come back in our lifetime. We will probably be too tired to enjoy them. The entire world goes through peaks and challenges. The exhilaration of the peaks is so wonderful, but they can't go on. When life reaches the top, it often falls. We can't be so sure of the future. Like the impact of the thirteenth-century plague caused by rats and fleas in Europe, the country will be different when this is over. Black Lives Matter will change some of the thinking. I hope there will be increased awareness and a push for racial justice. I'm worried that the divisions in our country are so frightening. There may even be a backlash. Many different ways of thinking will come out of this terrible trial. I hope they will be for the better.

I have been listening to the Metropolitan Opera every night. It is so good of the Met to present free performances via computers during this terrible time. I am so grateful that I had the chance to compare two versions of *Il Trovatore*, one German and one from the Metropolitan. My favorite stars were in the Metropolitan: Anna Netrova, Dmitri

Hvorostovsky, Delora Zajick, and Yonghoon Lee. The scenery of this production was often simple and very beautiful, and the "Anvil Chorus" was presented traditionally, just as I have seen it many times before. I loved it. It was Dmitri Hvorostovsky's first return in years after a brain-tumor operation. He looked older, but he sang beautifully and was so grateful to be back. The audience gave him a huge ovation. Norman and I had heard the young tenor, Yonghoon Lee, in New York about five years ago when he first started at the Met. We remember him singing "Don Jose" in *Carmen*.

The German presentation was wild. We had seen a production like it in Berlin. I wanted to see it because I had heard so much about Jonas Kaufman, the tenor. At first, I thought it was too distracting. I saw half of it before my computer cut off on Tuesday morning. When I streamed the Met's *Trovatore* that night, I liked the Met production better. The next day, I watched the entire German production of *Trovatore* and searched for my aunt's librettos. I read the whole story, which I had forgotten, and all of a sudden the German production made sense to me on several levels. It was done in black and white, with 1920s clothes, plus strange additions including a naked woman and a bloody baby, men sitting around below the stage, and strange dancers representing a psychiatric inner life. The busy set resembled an assemblage and the "Anvil" chorus was a bang on a huge oil barrel-like machine with a top-hatted nude dancer on top. It was quite an education. After seeing them both, I couldn't tell which presentation was better. When I turned on the traditional *Traviata*, I couldn't stand it after seeing the two wonderful productions of *Il Trovatore*.

We watched a different production almost every night. The operas were all good, especially *Carmen* and *The Daughter of the Regiment*. I had seen the production of *The Daughter of the Regiment* before with a much younger Dmitri Hvorostovsky. I really was excited to see modern operas I hadn't seen before, like Shostakovich's *The Nose* and *Satyagraha* by Philip Glass.

My backyard garden is an opulent opera with the daffy, dancing daffodils as the chorus line, the cherry tree the back curtain. The alizarin azalea is the devious diva singing a sparkling, springtime song to the tender tenor, the charming camellia. The birch trees above the camellias are the softly, swaying supernumeraries.

The cherry tree on our path exploded with a fluttering umbrella of plump, pink blossoms above its thin, twisted trunk. Three days later the spectacular show was gone, like the Japanese belief, *Ono No Aware*, of the spring trees blossoming, peeking, then disappearing in the rain. Like the beautiful trees, nothing is forever.

The tree is suddenly sprouting leaves. The drooping, dusty daffodils that were dancing a slow waltz in the wind became faded, dead or drunken hobos resting on the long, straight green weeds. They gave way to clumps of short, wistful, white iris with yellow tongue-like centers, lining the curving cement paths we walk every day. They are adding diurnally to the riot of red, white, blue, and purple flowers and foliage of the small bushes, plants, and wildflowers that constantly change as we pass. We walk by fields of wild grass and homesites planned out and waiting to be built. We look down long, paved driveways and pass large mansions that we never knew existed. Now we have time to see the wonder of it all and share it together. We feel lucky.

The stock market doesn't interest me. It can go up and it can go down. I worry about sickness and a recession. San Francisco will never be the same. My garden is blooming, the weather is summery, (we'll regret it this summer), and my family is fine, loving, and happy with their lives and careers. We are walking in our beautiful neighborhood, and it is all I can do to keep my husband from playing tennis in this terrible time.

I've contributed to my community. I've escorted three tours to France and one to China. I've read great books. We've hosted foreign students in our home. I have three healthy, grown children. I've watched my eight grandchildren grow, graduate, mature, travel, marry, divorce, and have children. I've painted for over forty years. I am now enjoying writing.

We say hi to so many neighbors and exchange friendly greetings as we walk the beautiful path outside our home. I can't believe the young women with strollers who see my gray hair and my husband's baldness and offer to shop for us. I connected with a neighbor who offered to walk with me when my husband is tired. I feel like I have returned to my small Idaho town, where everyone was friendly and helpful whenever there was a need.

Now, but four weeks into COVID-19, my husband and I are still healthy, thanks to the caring people around us who have offered food, distant visits, and hope. Our temple, Temple Isaiah, has been very supportive, with offers of help, classes, and sermons on Zoom. I am able to keep up with my writing class and my book group. Everything else I loved is postponed until the virus is over. My greatest hope is that I can have a big celebration of our two birthdays with Doctor Brian on March fourth next year.

June 2020

Printed in the United States
by Baker & Taylor Publisher Services